The History of Conversion
and Contemporary Cults

American University Studies

Series VII
Theology and Religion

Vol. 43

PETER LANG
New York · Bern · Frankfurt am Main · Paris

Natalie Isser and
Lita Linzer Schwartz

The History of Conversion
and Contemporary Cults

PETER LANG
New York · Bern · Frankfurt am Main · Paris

Library of Congress Cataloging-in-Publication Data

Isser, Natalie.
    The history of conversion and contemporary cults / Natalie Isser
and Lita Linzer Schwartz.

    p. cm.—(American university studies. Series VII, Theology
and religion ; vol. 43)
    Bibliography: p.
    1. Cults—United States. 2. Conversion. I. Schwartz, Lita
Linzer. II. Title. III. Series: American university studies.
Series VII, Theology and religion ; v. 43.
BL2525.I87   1988
291.4'2—dc19
ISBN 0-8204-0645-7   87-30974
ISSN 0740-0446   CIP

CIP-Titelaufnahme der Deutschen Bibliothek

Isser, Natalie:
The history of conversion and contemporary
cults / Natalie Isser and Lita Linzer Schwartz. –
New York; Bern; Frankfurt am Main; Paris:
Lang, 1988.
   (American University Studies: Ser. 7,
   Theology and Religion; Vol. 43)
   ISBN 0-8204-0645-7

NE: Schwartz, Lita Linzer:; American University
Studies / 07

© Peter Lang Publishing, Inc., New York 1988

Printed by Weihert-Druck GmbH, Darmstadt, West Germany

TABLE OF CONTENTS

PREFACE

As an outgrowth of research begun several years ago on antisemitism during the French Second Empire, we became enmeshed in the accounts of missionary activities of the churchmen of the period. What especially captured our attention in the narrations of various scandals involving several kinds of conversion were the accounts of "brainwashing" techniques similar to those applied in the Korean War and allegedly in today's cult groups. In contrast to these episodes, we also encountered genuine cases of intellectual conversion, such as that of Theodore Ratisbonne, and the mystical vision of Alphonse Ratisbonne, which was discussed by several eminent psychologists at the turn of the century. The various modes of proselytization and conversion came to fascinate us. As we continued our studies, these cases appeared analagous to many present–day conversions, illustrating the continuity of patterns of human behavior.

Nineteenth century France represented a period of rapid change, secularization, and a diminution of old values and customs, parallels to which we find in our own society. It was an environment, especially among the better educated, that provoked doubt, anxiety, and at times alienation. Religious proselytization was zealously pursued by both Protestants and Catholics, and their respective rates of success were relatively high with each other, though less so among Jews who were among their favored targets.

Impressed by the proliferation of cults and the enormous growth of preaching by evangelical sects in today's environment, we became sensitive to the similarities, despite the disparities, of the two eras. Our curiosity was piqued, and we were virtually propelled into a study of conversion and proselytization as a sociological and psychological phenomenon.

Many aspects of our research have already been reported in paper presentations at scholarly meetings and in articles in professional journals. These efforts would not have been possible without the support of our Campus administrators who supplied us with both research time and travel funds. The Faculty Scholarship Suppport Fund of The Pennsylvania State University provided funds which made possible the purchase of microfilm and other support services. We are also deeply indebted to the Library staff at the Ogontz Campus who secured printed materials, no matter how esoteric or remote the source.

In addition, we have had the benefit of working with a number of colleagues on various aspects of the research. Dr. Florence W. Kaslow, formerly of Hahnemann Medical College and now in private practice, and Jacqueline L. Zemel, an attorney in private practice, each brought her expertise to bear on portions of the work dealing with the cult movement. Vincent Virgulti, another colleague, was kind enough to translate Volli's work on the Mortara case from the original Italian. Dr. Patricia Rizzolo, a colleague in the English Department, read an early draft with a critical eye on the flow of ideas and on the correctness of our grammar. Margaret Taylor was our typist par excellence on earlier drafts of the manuscript.

Finally, our families have patiently endured our lengthy involvement with this project and with each other as we worked on it, with some members even accompanying us (enthusiastically) to Rome, Jerusalem, and Paris in order that we might complete our research. To all of them, our sincere gratitude for their roles in bringing this work into being.

N.I.

L.L.S.

Ogontz Campus
The Pennsylvania State University

INTRODUCTION

There are a number of approaches that may be taken to a study of proselytization, conversion, and commitment. Sociologists are primarily concerned with the organization and functioning of groups such as the "new religious movements" or cults that are discussed at some length in this work. Their focus is on practices that characterize a particular group or that are necessary to ensure its viability. Theologians tend to be more concerned with the belief system of a group. Is it mono– or multi–theistic? What obligations and rituals derive from the belief system? Historians may examine the development of a particular group over time or use the tenor of an era to explain why a specific group arose at a specific time. Psychologists are more apt to probe the relationship between individuals and the total group membership, impact of the belief systems on the individual, and psychological changes within the individual that enable him/her to adapt to and survive in a new environment (whether a group or a religion). We have chosen the last two approaches as cores of our work.

A second comment is necessary to "set the stage" for what is to come. We are well aware that there are developmental stages in the "life–cycle" of cults. Most start slowly, with few members, and grow when external conditions make it appear that the group has all the answers for certain social, economic, political, existential, or other questions. Other events may cause further modifications, such as the Jonestown tragedy, molestation of saffron–clad

Hare Krishna solicitors in airports or elsewhere; legal
pressures to change practices or be "persecuted." In general,
literature published up to or through 1980 often is more
extreme in tone, whether pro– or anti–cult, than more recent
literature. Therefore, interpretations of findings, responses to
stereotypes, and reactions to events must be considered in
the context of a particular point in time and often in terms of
a specific group rather than all groups.

The "heyday" of the cults came in the tumultuous decade
1965–75, when many changes occurred in American society.
They continued to flourish in the late 1970's, with an abrupt
and probably unwanted glare of negative publicity that
followed the Jonestown tragedy in November 1978 at least
partly causing a decline that is still in progress. To a
generation of youth shocked by a presidential assassination,
confronted with the need to make choices from an
abundance of life options, and caught up in the conflicts of
and surrounding the Viet Nam War, "opting out" via the
goal–oriented, regimented cults seemed — perhaps
unconsciously — a desirable alternative. Many youths were
seeking magical, authoritative answers to questions loosely
formulated in their minds. Cult recruiters, widely dispersed
on college campuses and wherever else youths were to be
found, provided facile answers and multiple assurances of
the individual's worth to offset his self–doubts.

What was objectionable was not the group's belief
system, or even its use as a "shelter" for the confused and
depressed, but the deception employed in recruiting and
fund–raising. Proselytization is not a new phenomenon. It is
central to the growth and maintenance of a cult group and is
an integral part of Christian and Western religious tradition.

Historical examination proves pertinent by revealing that the techniques and attitudes are not exclusively modern phenomena. While some cults are a twentieth–century manifestation, their recruitment — whether aggressive as in the early phases or more conventional as in the present — are deeply rooted not only in quintessentially American evangelical tradition, but also in the Western Christian mainstream religious experience.

CHAPTER I — REVIEWING THE CONCEPTS

Man's sense of impotence before the overwhelming majesty of nature and the entire creative process has resulted in his sense of religiosity: a universal phenomenon among all social units in every place and at all times. How we define religion, however, is difficult, for people express their reverence in as many ways as they do all their social activities.

Religious behavior and ritual solidifies the social order by establishing rules and institutions that ensure civility and create moral statutes binding human beings together. It disciplines social relationships, and it provides vehicles through which people can express collective affection and loyalty.

Moreover, religious behavior and/or faith also satisfy certain psychological needs. It provides explanations for the supernatural and the enormity of the universe. It also produces solace, comfort, and reassurance in the face of tragedy which confronts us all. The promise of eternal life enables people to face death with more equanimity; it helps people grapple with guilt, and it sometimes gives people parental figures to whom they can turn for help and love when confronted by harsh realities. Religion can offer transcendental avenues of escape from the ennui and frustrations of daily life.

Religion also creates an institutional framework through which individuals can move through the passages of life collectively: the induction of the young into the adult community; marriage which legitimizes the family, and conversely divorce; the celebration of birth; and comfort during bereavement.

In sum, religion creates morality and ethics for society and the individual, encompassing within its system of values and responsibilities a framework of reality that establishes man's relationship to the universe. Therefore, no historical, sociological, or psychological study can ignore the impact of religious belief, institutional loyalties, and the individual's commitment to these various ideals. Nor is it strange that, despite the prevalence and triumph of a secular and materialistic culture, millions of Americans remain enthusiastically loyal to an enormous variety of religious and cultic groups.

Many have found modern beliefs wanting in providing comfort, succor, and support in the variety of life crises faced by everyone. Hence, the nineteenth as well as the present century has witnessed a burgeoning of religious movements, missionary groups, and alternative religious sects in both the United States and Western Europe. As one writer eloquently declared, "The great mysteries of birth and death, of passion in love and hate, of hope and despair, dreams and disappointments are missing in their philosophy [secular humanism]... . The secular religions have failed and are failing man, leaving him, individually and socially, despairing while the organizations leave him organized but lonely, and his spirit frustrated and dismayed searches

through the encircling gloom for one gleam of kindly light"
(Thompson, 1946, p.597).

American cultural tradition has always contained a
history of communal settlements, of religious sectarianism,
and peculiar cults. Part of the reason lies in the unusual
social and economic dynamics of the American scene - the
constantly shifting frontier, the structural weakness of
establishment religions, the evangelical forces produced by a
more democratic society, and the very mobility of the
American community itself. To orient our study
appropriately, it is necessary to examine this background
more closely, defining certain terms and providing
perspective and context for the reader.

Communes

The study of communes is usually in the province of
sociologists, although historians have also found them to be
of interest as phenomena in specific eras. It is only in recent
years that psychologists have attended to these groups,
mostly in terms of who joins them and the psychodynamics
of the groups. This attention has expanded as a result of the
great growth of communes, and cults, in the past fifteen to
twenty years. Zablocki defines a commune as:

> any group of five or more adult individuals (plus children if
> any)the majority of whose dyads are *not cemented by blood or
> marriage*, who have decided to live together, *without compulsion,
> for an indefinite period of time*, primarily for the sake of an
> *ideological goal*, focused upon the *achievement of community*, for
> which a collective household is deemed essential (1980, p.7).

The commune has a public identity; that is, a name and/or function known to the larger society, but there are several types of communes. They differ in ideology and in structure, as well as in their durability.

> Eastern religious communes stress self-discipline as a means of developing inner harmony. The guru (teacher-leader) generally has unquestioned authority, and there is "a preoccupation with ideological matters and a perceived unanimity of belief unmatched in other communes" as well as a "sense of collective separateness from the world" (Zablocki & Aidala, 1980, p.238).

Christian religious communes attempt to re-establish traditional fundamental Christian values, and are typically conservative in their social and political orientation. Psychological communes, by contrast, focus on finding the hidden perfect self within each individual. Its members, more alienated from society than members of other types of communes, according to Zablocki and Aidala, find that the heavy emphasis on individualism appears to be as much a defense against their feelings of worthlessness and purposelessness as against the society that they blame for bringing out the worst in people. Other types of communes include those that perceive themselves as prototypes of alternative family structures and those that are countercultural, seeking utopian changes in society (although there tends to be some disagreement as to what constitutes Utopia and what changes are desirable).

Kanter (1972) similarly views communes in terms of voluntary commitment to the values and goals of the group, identity as a physical and social entity, but adds the factor of **shared** resources and finances. She differentiated three types of communes: religious (e.g., Oneida Community, Shakers,

Hutterites); politico-economic (Owen's New Harmony, Modern Times, Llano Colony); and psychosocial ("hippie" communes, Walden Two, Synanon). The psychosocial communes of the 1960's and 1970's combined elements of the countercultural and psychological types differentiated by Zablocki and Aidala (*supra*). In Kanter's view, the three underlying reasons for establishing communes have much in common.

They reject the established order as sinful, unjust, or unhealthy. They stress the possibility of perfection through restructuring social institutions. They seek the recreation of a lost unity — between man and God, between man and man, or between man and himself. They stress immediacy, the opportunity to achieve such harmonies now. They frequently seek a return to the land as the pathway to perfection. And they often lead to a single development: the utopian community or commune (1972, p.8).

In the mid-nineteenth century as in the 1960's, communes were focused on one or more of the following: social issues, religious revivalism, dissatisfaction with capitalism, or concern with individual fulfillment. The anti-capitalism or Utopian emphasis is closest to those modern groups that Shupe and Bromley (1980) describe as "world-saving," while the individual fulfillment communes most closely resemble the narcissistic quasi-therapy groups, or Eastern-oriented cults, common in the 1970's and early 1980's, some of which may not be communal in life-style. We might also cite the prototypical Israeli kibbutz as Utopian in nature, although there are variations today even among kibbutzim in religiosity, child-rearing philosophies and practices, and life-style.

Rural communes, such as those described by E.M. Levine (1980b), were a countercultural, areligious, idealistic phenomenon of the 1960's. Their members tried, often unsuccessfully, to create a utopia in which both social equality and self-actualization could flourish. Although their middle-class, well-educated members rejected urban life and middle-class strivings, most neither totally rejected their families and benefits received from them, nor did they gain total independence from the products and services of the broader society. Living in a communal residence was totally voluntary, but also so self-centered an existence that most of these communes could not survive. Levine (1980b) points out that the prevalent narcissism was most clearly seen in communal child-rearing practices or, more accurately, the absence of any systematic supervisory, guidance, or developmental pattern of child-rearing. This is atypical of communes of the nineteenth century and of the more religiously-oriented communes of today, both of which are characterized by considerable attentiveness to their children's upbringing in the ideology of the group.

Of considerable importance in these several definitions of communes is the emphasis on voluntary, informed choice to become a member. The significance of this point will become apparent as we discuss conversion in later chapters. A second point emphasized is the strength of commitment to the commune, which is also highly relevant to our study.

Religion

There are many ways to define religion — in terms of its meaning to an individual, in legal terms, in varying theological terms, in terms of its organizational structure, and so on. Unquestionably, religion means different things to different people. From a sociological point of view, religion has four principal aspects: 1) it is concerned with what is regarded as sacred; 2) it has a system of beliefs and practices related to what is considered sacred; 3) it is group–rather than individual–oriented in activity and belief; and 4) it deals with problems of ultimate meaning (Chalfont, Beckley, & Palmer, 1981, p.28).

From an idiosyncratic point of view, of course, there may be variation even within a single religion as to the depth of belief and the scope of activity. Between religions, there are differences in what specifically is held sacred, and also in resolutions to existential questions. One religion may focus on life in the "hereafter" and another on behavior in the "here and now." Nevertheless, virtually all groups purporting to be religions do have the elements described above in common. They also have consequences for the individual in the conduct of daily life.

Our study, which deals with conversion from one religion to another, does not reject the commonality of elements but does focus in part on the psychological effects of moving from one system of beliefs and practices to a different set. Although several of our case studies involve two of the major mainstream religions, we also consider cults, some of which are religious in nature and some of which are not but may claim to be in order to be protected by the First Amendment to the Constitution. Thus, religious sectarianism plays a significant role in the chapters to come.

Cults

The term "cult" may be distinguished from the term "sect" by sociologists according to many criteria, and is viewed by some of them as a pejorative term. As noted above, however, not all cults are religious in nature, although those that are tend to vary considerably both among themselves and as compared with denominations and sects. One widely accepted definition of a cult includes the following specifications:

> It is a group which follows a dominant leader, often living, who may make absolute claims that he is divine, God incarnate, the messiah, or God's emissary, and that he is omniscient and infallible. Membership is contingent on complete and literal acceptance of the leader's claims and acceptance of his doctrines and dogma. Complete, unquestioning loyalty and allegiance are demanded together with a total willingness to obey the cult leader's commands without question — which may include a unique way of viewing the world, of acting, of dressing, or of thinking (S.V.Levine, 1980, pp.123-124).

In addition, Levine, a psychiatrist, found the groups he studied to share such aspects as charismatic leadership, rituals,

> a quasi-intellectual theological tone, rigid hierarchy and rules, relative ascetism, high-powered fund-raising techniques or tithes, and houses of worship ... the particular content of the theology is never as important as the trappings, and certainly not nearly as significant as believing, belonging, and the increase in self-esteem (S.V.Levine, 1980, p.125).

The cults in some cases resemble Eastern-type communes, Hare Krishna ashrams and Children of God "colonies" being two examples. In other instances, they take the stance of psychological communes without necessarily having all members live in communal residences. The Church of Scientology, the Divine Light Mission, and some quasi-therapeutic groups that are cult-like, represent this type. Unlike Kanter's view of communes (*supra*), however, members of cults rarely share equally in resources and finances with the leadership.

One chapter of our study is focused solely on proselytization and conversion as related to the cult movement. Parts of other chapters are devoted to the related effects of cult membership on individuals, their families, and the community.

As Ostow observes, movements such as the cults repudiate reality — social, temporal, and spiritual. They are, in his view,

> deviant, or rebellious, or heretical. Being derived from personal "revelation" rather than conventionally recognized tradition, they are essentially antinomian. They secede from, or attempt to take over, current social organization. Those that are more realistic may succeed; very few do. Those that are less realistic usually fail, so that we hear little or nothing of them in the annals of history (Ostow, 1982, p.248).

From an historical perspective, this is a valid statement as one can see in examining communities of the past, although some of the earlier communes were more socialistic than religious in orientation (e.g., Icarist, Fourist, Owenites). These groups were representative of an idealistic drive to achieve an egalitarian and more democratic society. Many of these groups created in microcosm a society that rejected mainstream religious beliefs and created an alternative moral and civil group which involved strong binding interpersonal relationships of the members. The more lasting groups forced or committed their members to some type of sacrifice, investment (of time and goods), renunciation of their present existence, communion with the group, total immersion of self to the new belief and finally transcendance in the conviction of both temporal and spiritual salvation. Most cults, like the communal groups, purport to give their members security that satisfies idealistic yearning plus a vital religious message within a prophetic tradition. However, in too many cases in the past, as now, these colonies did not and do not provide such spiritual sustenance. They frequently deny educational opportunities, hamper or deny individual choices, and prevent the intrusion of what they call "worldly" ideas. They thus become provincial, inward-oriented, mercenary settlements little concerned with their fellow men and social problems, obsessed principally with recruitment or fund-raising to enhance the prestige of the leader or the colony.

One historian illustrates that analogy by comparing the House of David and the Koreshan cult, both of the late nineteenth century, and David Berg's Children of God — a contemporary group. Each claimed that it represented the only true moral path; they were and are lead by charismatic leaders; they established communal societies; they rejected the secular world because of its corruption. They had and still developed their own peculiar sexual behaviors that are subject to the total control of the community (Fogarty, 1981, 130-146).

David Berg's group had and has special appeal for the runaway, the addict — those who are already rejected by their families, or feel as though they have been rejected. They revere Berg as their King David or Moses; their moral codes are based on Biblical fundamentalism, and sexual patterns follow the proclivities of Berg himself. In the past, Purnell, of the Koreshan sect, occupied the same position in his cult, as did Joseph Smith in the Mormon faith, and others in theirs (Harrison, 1979). Members turn over all their possessions to David; they reject their families to live in the commune. They eschew their individual choices, subject themselves to public confession and accept a non-private sexual life (Enroth, Ericson, & Peters, 1972; Enroth, 1977). All of these characteristics were evident in many of the millenarian movements of the past.

To ensure proper reverence for the leader, and to be certain that members fulfill their financial obligations, the communal leaders demand total obedience and submersion of the recruit into the collective life-style. Therefore, indoctrination and isolation were and are used to maintain a high degree of enthusiasm and to imbue the recruit with animus for the more conventional life.

A common thread that is observed both in the historical analysis of past cults as well as contemporary ones — whether they were and are manipulative, self serving, or psychologically damaging — was and is the enormous hold that the prophet or leader possesses over his disciples, who, in turn, dedicate their lives to him, his colony, and the tenets that emanate from both. Further, all religious principles are fed upon his hopes, his fears, and the religious principles extant at the time.

Purnell, a prophet of the Koreshan sect in New York at the end of the nineteenth century, selected a medley of religious themes popular in that state, just as the Millerites and Joseph Smith activated millenarian dreams of the nineteenth century (Harrison, 1979). Father Divine in the 1930's spoke to Black despair and thwarted aspirations in Harlem and the Philadelphia slums (Harris, 1954). David Berg appealed to the disinherited hippies of the 1960's; Jones preached racial and economic equality, and the Reverend Moon promised redemption through family service as so eagerly desired by the earnest idealistic adolescent (Fogarty, 1981). Religious leaders drew upon already existing theological and social doctrines, redefined them to fit their needs, developed a communal society which provided a sense of family and a reordered social network, which thus provided for salvation in both this world and the next. These cults filled a void, and created a new cosmos, which gave a sense of purpose to those who were seeking a new transcendentalism (Tipton, 1982).

As we examine proselytization, conversion, and commitment against the context of communes, religions, and cults, we can illustrate both abundant similarities and painful realities.

Conversion

Religious conversion once occupied an important role in the varied writings of such early social scientists as G. Stanley Hall, Edwin Starbuck, William James, George Coe, Clarence Leuba, and Morton Prince. The majority of cases in the late nineteenth and early twentieth centuries about which they wrote were focused on sudden conversions of the type occurring at revival meetings. Much of the literature of that era was filled with histories of lapsed Christians returning to the fold (today's "born again" Christians), or sinners such as alcoholics being redeemed or reformed. That subject was largely abandoned as a source of significant research in the more secular and scientific middle years of the twentieth century.

However, the tragedy of Jonestown in late 1978, the continuing anguish of concerned parents and their struggle against a proliferating number of non-conventional cults or "deviant religions," and the renewed religious fervor of the more aggressive evangelical Christian sects have once more impelled social and behavioral scientists to reexamine the process of conversion and its psychological and social ramifications. Many studies, therefore, have appeared since the late 1970's dealing with sudden conversion to the cult movements of recent decades.

Conversion incorporates a number of elements, the most notable being proselytization and commitment. Proselytization is a frequent precursor of conversion, although it may be subtle or intense. Commitment is a hallmark of true conversion and may be demonstrated in a number of ways. These elements, and the concept of conversion itself, are the focus of our study.

Scholarly interest in conversion has not been without conflict, however. The conflict has resulted from the publication of disparate points of view, especially between those who accept converts' narratives about their pre-conversion motives at face value and those who question the validity of such recollections. Disputes arise particularly in

18

cases where an individual espouses one faith or no faith one day, and has made a dramatic and therefore startling reversal to intense belief or a new belief the next day. Somewhat less attention has been paid to other types of religious conversion and the psychodynamics underlying them.

Conversion as change

Conversion means change: exchange of one currency for another, alteration in attitudes or beliefs, and, more to the point here, transfer of religious identification and adaptation to a newly adopted religious faith. If the conversion involved simply a change of opinion and value systems from one faith or ideology to another and was a rational intellectual and private act, little examination of the phenomenon would be needed. In fact, however, most conversions, even under the most rational circumstances, not only produce marked psychological effects upon the individual, but also upon his or her family. The act of conversion may signify the denial of a past identity with the assumption of a new one; it may mean, as the individual moves from one value system to another, the necessity of resolving deeply felt cognitive dissonances. Hence, incompatible beliefs, and the conflicts created by them, must be resolved so that the individual can commit himself to faith. Interfaith conversion, in effect, does involve "a rejection of some normative system with the attribution of legitimacy to some other set of associations and norms" (Parucci, 1968, p.149). Christians, however, "who cross denominational lines do not have to surrender basic identification with the Christian religion" (Appel, 1969, p.118). This is obviously not true for Jews who convert to

Christianity, for acceptance of Jesus' divinity or as messiah is incompatible with Jewish belief.

Religious conversion is clearly a major step in the life of an individual. It can, for example, be the outcome of wrestling with major psychological problems originating in some phase of the development of personality, with the act of conversion being the extraordinary means by which the individual achieves great accomplishment in her/his new identity (Erikson, 1950; Gillespie, 1979; Isser & Schwartz, 1980a). However, one must accept this view with caution, for "The individual who seeks resolution of psychic conflict through religious affiliation is prone to become disaffected with one religious community after another as each eventually fails to satisfy unconscious needs" (Spero, 1980, p.163). Another possibility is that the conversion experience can be destructive, inducing guilt (Isser, 1979), or, as in the case of modern cult movements, the modification of personal growth patterns. Conversion used as an escape may be one method of attempting to resolve guilt-laden conflicts with parents or other family members. There is, after all, no more effective method of denial or rejection than to convert to a "deviant religion" or to one antithetical to the original faith, thereby repudiating the past teachings and more traditional orientation of the family.

The new religion may provide a new father-image who assumes the role of "good" authoritarian parent — the opposite of the "evil" one rejected by the youth — to the individual whose conversion is rooted in unresolved adolescent conflict directed against the father. Less often, the new religion may offer a mother figure proffering the maternal love denied by a cold, "wicked-witch" mother.

Conversion may unconsciously be the means by which the young person punishes his family as he seeks revenge for his hurts. Alternatively, the latter behavior may be reflected in other ways that may be equally unacceptable to the family — as in the choice of a spouse, vocation, or friends. At times, some cults attract young people who are acting upon self-rejection and seeking an appropriate type of self-punishment. This often results in their joining ascetic communes or embarking upon a monastic life. This choice may also be predicated upon the desire to escape from decision-making, responsibility, or even from the obligations of sexuality (Eichorn, 1965, p.20).

However, we must be wary of viewing "conversion" only as a means of resolving cognitive dissonance or of establishing new identities as a cure-all for festering and destructive neuroses. We must also recognize that it may be the expression of repressed resentment and/or hatred toward the father (Scroggs & Douglas, 1977); finding a solution to the questions of one's existence (Ferm, 1959); desire to conform, usually for the sake of family unity (Gordon, 1967); and feelings of guilt, remorse, fear, consolation, or gratitude (Underwood, 1925). There is frequent overlap of cause expressed by authors discussing these psychodynamics of conversion. The weight of opinion, however, is with those who see unconscious rather than conscious factors as playing a significant role in conversion (Scroggs & Douglas, 1977, p.261). Among the latter would be both Sigmund Freud and William James.

As a contemporary phenonmenon, conversion is prevalent in modern societies not because of the sudden efflorescence of new religions or semi-mystical cults, but because, in highly mobile societies with sophisticated media, identities tend to be less firmly rooted in traditional roles and assignments. Families tend to be separate from their familiar roots and networks, and family members tend more and more to be in diverse pursuits throughout the day. In addition, it has become easier for individuals to become acquainted with a variety of alternative life-styles and cultures that are frequently enticing or exotic, or which offer an escape from dreary realities. Furthermore, the teaching and spread in belief of cultural relativity often eases the paths to such conversions (Berger, Berger, & Kellner, 1973, pp.48-49).

Foundations of conversion experiences

No matter what type of conversion is studied, the researcher is confronted with ambiguity and the need for critical assessment of the individual's account of his experience. Autobiographical reports of converts' experiences generally are plausible but somewhat unreliable. The events and emotions preceding the experience, whether a gradual rational or a sudden emotional event, are related **after** the alternation of identity and in the context of the new values and new personal commitments. Frequently, the clue is in the language used (Beckford, 1978). That is, for example, members of the same religious movement tend to use the same words and phrases in expressing themselves about the past and about their new-found sources of faith. For the individual, the past is constantly changing and malleable as it is continuously reinterpreted and reexamined when present perceptions are altered. Conversion provides a significant opportunity for the reassessment of personal biography, as the need to explain and justify the change of identity leads to the rationalization that one's entire life was a preparation for the final moment of revelation that came with the new religious experience. This can be explained in either rational or mystical terms, as in the accounts of St. Augustine or Cardinal Newman (c.f. Berger, Berger, & Kellner, 1973, pp.57, 61) or in the cases of Theodore and Alphonse Ratisbonne (Isser & Schwartz, 1980c).

Given the possibility that sudden conversion, especially, is often a highly emotional experience, the researcher needs to question whether the post facto autobiographical reports are "justificatory rather than explanatory" (Wallis, 1979, p.6). Or, as Toch put it:

> The changes that follow the act of conversion are directed at the task of consolidating psychological gains. As soon as new beliefs are adopted, a stock-taking follows, which records the advantage of the new beliefs over the old. Simultaneously, the reinterpretation of reality begins. Old facts are given new meanings (1965,p.127). Unfortunately, we rarely have available pre-conversion data that might reduce ambiguities and contradictions, such as anecdotal school records, projective test protocols, personal diaries, or even family films.

Conversion should also be examined within a broader sociological context. Although the individual's choice may disturb and upset his family and associates, he may accept a new faith initially because of the socialization and acceptance of a peer group. Missionaries are most effective, for example, when interpersonal relationships create vital bonds and whole new social and quasi-familial networks. Once the individual submerges himself in these new and vital relationships, he can subsequently absorb readily the ideology of alternate beliefs (Stark & Bainbridge, 1980). Case studies of historical conversions reinforce the evidence of such "social networks" evident in proselytization techniques used today not only by the Mormons and Jehovah's Witnesses, but even more effectively by various cults.

Vulnerability to conversion

There appear to be two age periods at which conversion is most likely to occur among those whose conversions resulted from proselytization. Hall (1904) was among the earliest to identify adolescence as one such critical point. The search for an "identity," the desire for commitment conflicting with ambivalent feelings toward the traditional (and therefore counter-individualizing) ties of the family to its religion, and heightened suggestibility as the youth is exposed to a greater diversity of viewpoints, are among the factors cited in support of the high rate of conversion among adolescents. Although others writing in Hall's period similarly found adolescence to be a crucial time for conversion, it should be noted that adolescence in America today is prolonged into what is legally adulthood, that is, into the early twenties.

The other life stage at which conversions seem to occur with increased frequency is middle life, as the individual approaches and faces the crisis of integrity about his past years (Erikson, 1950; Scroggs & Douglas, 1977). Concern with whether one has lived a constructive life or whether one's life might yet be made more meaningful through a change in orientation can precipitate conversion at this later age. The resulting inner debate is often crystallized by the declamations of evangelical orators, with predictable results.

Historical evidence supports these theories and those of
Margaret Singer (1979b), who declared that anyone engaged
in an internalized emotional crisis, such as the need for
making a crucial decision, loneliness, alienation, or a deep-
seated disappointment, was vulnerable to proselytization.
Examples of this type of conversion were reported frequently
in nineteenth-century France. Individuals who were ill or
dying in Catholic hospitals were especially vulnerable. As
examples, one can cite a young soldier, Braun Gerson, who
was baptized by a visiting priest and nuns in Marseille (AN
F19, 9, 16 January 1860); an elderly doctor, Doctor Terquem,
who was converted on his death bed (AN F19, 11031, 19
March 1845); and a young mother, Mrs. Wurmser, who was
not only baptized herself, but also committed her children to
the care of Abbé Theodore Ratisbonne to be educated as
Catholics (T. Ratisbonne, I, 1905). Furthermore, Jewish
newspapers of the time complained that missionary activity
in France and England was directed primarily to children or
adolescents who had little ability to defend themselves
(*London Jewish Chronicle*, 21 August 1857, 21 January 1853, 13
May 1853, 5 October 1854, 27 September 1854, 20 February
1854; *Verité Israelité*, 24 October 1861). One editor declared:
"The conversionists prey upon the young and the poor, and
through very slow and very gradual persuasion tempt them"
(*London Jewish Chronicle*, 30 January 1857, 6 February 1867),
and another editor admonished Jewish parents to distrust
governesses and other instructors, and to maintain a
continuous vigilance over the activities of their young
(*London Jewish Chronicle*, 6 March 1867, 3 April 1857). The
same sentiments were echoed by the Jewish papers of Paris
(*Univers Israélite*, April, May 1861; *Archives Israélites*, July,
August 1861).

Conversion models

There are three basic types of conversion: intellectual or gradual, and aggressive or sudden, both of which are viewed as internalized conformity; pro forma, which is seen as compliance without strong commitment; and a final form postulated by Parker (1978) as a "developmental" type related to adolescent crises, and which is neither intellectual nor traumatic. Whatever the type of conversion or the age at which it occurs, however, conversion brings drastic change to the life of the individual. Sobel (1974) goes so far as to assert that conversion is "wrenching and cataclysmic" in its effects on the person. This alteration is signaled, according to Travisano, "by a radical reorganization of identity, meaning, and life. The convert may be recognizable by his piety" (1970, p.600). Furthermore, due to these radical modifications, he is often regarded as a traitor by his former associates, compounding the psychological effects. In the case of the Jew who has converted to a Christian faith, he may become a marginal individual, not wholly accepted as an enthusiastic Christian by other Christians, and regarded by his former co-religionists as a renegade (Graebar & Britt, 1942, pp.68-69). The convert has embraced a "negative" identity, one antithetical to and often specifically prohibited by his original orientation. Having done so, he frequently becomes even more intense in his new affiliation than persons born to the faith he has adopted, perhaps as a measure of psychological self-defense.

Most researchers are primarily concerned with the drama of sudden conversion, but many describe and analyze those conversions that occur gradually as well. Some authors, notably Salzman (1966), regard the latter as progressive, maturational, and intellectual, in contrast to the regressive and/or psycho-pathological conversions that occur abruptly. The intellectual or gradual conversion can be the outcome of a prolonged and quite rational search for a solution to the individual's emotional needs (Ferm, 1959; Salzman, 1953, 1966). The intellectual convert perceives his new values and goals as being of a higher order than those he has abandoned. Having arrived at this determination through reason, he not only has convinced himself of the validity of it, but often seeks to convince others that his decision is justified not only for himself, but for them as well. Solely concerned with finding the one "true" religion, some of these types of converts are termed "authentic converts" by Gordon (1967). Glanz and Harrison (1978) found a similar degree of authenticity in students at Israeli yeshivot who had moved gradually from minimal observance of Jewish law and ritual to a new commitment as orthodox Jews. They regard this transformation, however, as an "alteration" of identity rather than a conversion, similar to Travisano's concept of "alternation" (1970). It is, put another way, an instance of "deviance via over-conformity" (Parrucci, 1968, p.145, n.2).

In a study of 49 converts, aged 15-26, Parker found that "gradual converts," as compared with "sudden" or "developmental" converts, were "less neurotic, display more mature identity patterns and have more positive religious home environments" (1978, p.3371-B). Kildahl (1965) had earlier found that gradual converts tended to be more intelligent and less hysterical or emotionally labile than sudden converts. Salzman (1966), too, found that the gradual conversion, which he termed progressive or maturational, occurred more often in reasonably "normal" people, and represented "the achievement of the ultimate in the humanistic religions — the positive fulfillment of one's powers with self-awareness, concern for others, and oneness with the world" (p.12). Although the spiritual journey implied in intellectual conversion may be undertaken because of a real philosophic void in an individual's life, it may also arise from an "unpleasant experience, real or fancied, that the proselyte has had with rabbi, priest, or minister. The feeling that his clergyman is a 'hypocrite,' dishonest intellectually, unethical, or immoral, is recorded in several... interviews with converts" (Gordon, 1967, p.3). Anger at a rabbi, for example, was the alleged reason for Disraeli's father having him and his siblings baptized into the Anglican Church.

Usually, the intellectual convert seeks information through formal or informal study, attendance at varied religious services or meetings, and discussions with persons learned in a particular faith or comparative religion. The more traditional religions, such as Catholicism and Judaism, tend to require such a period of study before formal conversion rites are permitted, for an internalized comprehension of the theology and its practices leads to a deeper and more enduring commitment than an impulsive or spontaneous conversion would. Often the intellectual convert can develop, as a result, more personal effectiveness in his new awareness, provided his conversion really resolves his earlier conflicts (T.Ratisbonne, I, 1905; Erikson, 1956).

Unlike the intellectual or gradual conversion, the impulsive conversion is viewed as being regressive and based on emotion rather than reason. The World War I cliché that "there are no atheists in the foxholes" is an illustration of the emotional, immature "bargaining" that occurs in times of personal crisis. Underwood (1925) stressed both fear and gratitude as motives for conversion — fear so pervasive that the individual resorts to religion almost superstitiously, and gratitude so overwhelming that the individual revives a dormant belief in the Almighty. Heirich alludes specifically to the "alliance with supernatural; forces that could change the power balance" (1977, p.656) as part of his theory that fantasy solutions to stress are one explanation for conversion. Also part of that approach is the changing of "one's frame of reference so that previously distressing material no longer seems important" (Heirich, 1977, p.656). An acceptance of the view that recovery from an illness or survival in a disaster is in the hands of an external supernatural force rather than the self only represents conversion, however, when the individual has previously been a non-believer.

Repeatedly in the literature on conversion, there are statements similar to Travisano's: "... conversion often involves a period of emotional upset and indecision during which the individual may become severely depressed or confused and may experience emotionally induced somatic upsets" (1970, p.600). Relief comes with the acceptance of the new belief. Salzman saw such a regressive resolution of problems as a "pseudo-solution ... likely to occur in neurotic, prepsychotic or psychotic persons, although it may also occur in presumably normal people when they are faced with major conflicts or insuperable difficulties" (1966, p.13). Streiker (1971), studying the Jesus Movement specifically, described the introspection, depression, confusion, and feelings of guilt as normal adolescent phenomena, part of the search for identity and direction. However, he also pointed out that most adults have learned to live with themselves, faults and all, while

> the self -dissatisfied young person does not try to make peace with himself but rather to escape from himself. He finds a better or ideal state of existence. Or he is born again.
>
> Religious conversion, romantic love, and enthusiasm for a cause are identical in this respect: they offer an opportunity for the individual to lose his limited self through union with a greater reality (Streiker, 1971, p.87).

This explanation echoes that of Coe (1900) eight decades earlier, and is supported by Wilson (1972) who had studied a group of white Protestant adults (N = 63, mean age = 42). His subjects reported that, at the time of their conversion experience, they were emotionally "empty" (44%), or confused (38%), or afraid (27%), or depressed (19%), or angry (6%). Only 30 percent of Wilson's subjects considered themselves psychologically normal at the time (1972, p.383). Nicholi similarly found that his subjects, although outwardly socially successful, "expressed dissatisfaction with their lives, especially in their relationships with others.... They expressed a profound loneliness and a 'sense of not belonging' " (1974, p. 397). As previously noted, such post facto reports "may be seen as products of [converts'] new identities rather than as objective reports on the antecedents of the conversion process" (Greil & Rudy, 1981, p.8).

Put in other terms by Morris and Morris, who also studied youthful converts, "Those *seeking access* to some great source of power are perhaps more externally locused, and thus have a lowered sense of their own inner life purpose, tending more to see purpose in external events or stimuli"

(1978, p.20). This, too, describes adolescents in turmoil who convert suddenly and intensely to a deeper or different religious faith. When Levine asked his cult member sample (N = 106) specifically what they gained from their new religion,

> "...spiritual, transcendental, or mystical rationales were less frequent (20 percent) than intrapsychic and interpersonal ones (80 percent). Seventy-seven cited a sense of security and feeling more self-confident. . . . all members reported closer, better, and more friends since joining - and a sense of belonging. Only after these reasons were given were spiritual issues discussed..."(1978, p. 79).

Many of the recent studies of sudden converts have been focused on members of the so-called "new religious movements" or "cults," or on the charismatic — "born-again" — Christians.

> The hysterical symptoms which accompany the extreme sudden convert's experience may indicate that possession of a suggestibility trait may facilitate the sudden conversion experience, although the link between suggestibility, hysteria, and extreme sudden conversion is not firmly established (Scobie, 1975, pp.111-112).

Such symptoms are frequently noted at religious revival meetings (Christenson, 1963) and in the cults. Scobie's hypothesis will be elaborated upon in the discussions of the sudden conversion of Alphonse Ratisbonne and of religious cult members.

Behavior subsequent to the emotional or regressive or mystical conversion similarly seems to follow a pattern. Salzman has delineated its characteristics:

"(1) The convert has an exaggerated, irrational intensity of belief in the new doctrine... (2) The convert is more concerned with the form and doctrine than with the greater principle of his new beliefs; (3) his attitude toward his previous belief is one of contempt, hatred and denial, and he rejects the possibility that there might be any truth in it; (4) he is intolerant toward all deviates, with frequent acting-out by denouncing and endangering previous friends and associates; (5) he shows a crusading zeal and a need to involve others by seeking new conversions; and (6) he engages in masochistic and sadistic activities, displaying a need for martyrdom and self-punishment" (1966, pp.18-19).

Such behavior is frequently seen among today's cult members, and was also observable in the post-conversion behavior of Theodore and Alphonse Ratisbonne; involuntary converts, like Edgardo Mortara, the Bluth sisters, and others to be discussed in later chapters rarely exhibited such a pattern.

Several authors have postulated two other themes involved in sudden conversion, particularly of young people. One is self-hatred, especially as aroused at revival meetings led by " 'hellfire and damnation' preachers who spout hate, **not** love, and inflame the congregation with threats of eternal damnation and with descriptions of the most vile and hateful consequences of sinfulness" (Salzman, 1966, p.17). An individual with an overly strict superego may magnify a minor weakness into a mortal sin in such an atmosphere. Or, having failed to reach his lofty goals or acted in keeping with his high ideals may, in the wake of such evangelistic chastisement, perceive his failures as glaring evidence of his sinful character. Beset by feelings of guilt and anxiety, he readily accepts the proffered salvation. Allison (1968) noted that certain similarities involving this pattern exist among

32

such diverse processes as faith healing, religious revivalism, thought reform, and psychotherapy, to all of which may be added "religious cults" such as those that have been spawned in recent decades.

It is instructive and interesting to examine Fromm's thoughts on self-hate of almost five decades ago in comparison with the attitudes (or platitudes) expressed toward the self today, thoughts that are relevant to the extremist position. On the one hand, we still say to young children, "Don't be selfish!", while on the other, adolescents and adults are exhorted to "Do your own thing!" According to Fromm, the individual was perceived from a Calvinist point of view, still widely held, as essentially wicked and powerless. "This emphasis on the nothingness and wickedness of the individual implies that there is nothing he should like about himself. This doctrine is rooted in contempt and hatred for oneself" (Fromm, 1939, p.508). This has not been a tenet basic to Judaism and, indeed, it contradicts the Judeo-Christian injunction to "love thy neighbor as thyself." The incompatibility of the two viewpoints is self-evident.

Nevertheless, closely related to the evangelically-aroused antecedent of sudden conversion is the motive of self-hatred. This may be personal, as when the individual rejects himself as unworthy and unlovable in the Calvinistic sense, or group-oriented, as sometimes occurs among members of minority groups. Not only does the individual who hates his group of origin accept the majority's stereotype of his compatriots, but he also adopts the majority's negative attitudes toward them. Kurt Lewin (1948) described this phenomenon as one in which the minority members of a society internalized the values of the dominant group and judged themselves accordingly. Prompted by persecution and exile at one extreme and mildly negative receptions at the other, some Jews in all centuries have exhibited behaviors strongly conformist to the dominant powers as a defense against criticism of their people and aggression against themselves. As part of such behavior, they have discriminated against their former brothers to demonstrate the strength of their new commitment to the prevailing philosophy or faith. [This phenomenon was also observed by Kenneth Clark in his early studies of Black children, who chose "white" rather than "Negro" dolls as "nice" (Clark,1963).]

In the case of the Messengers of the New Covenant, who call themselves "Hebrew Christians," for example, much personal testimony centers on alienation from and feelings of anomie toward Jews (Sobel, 1974). As Jews increasingly assimilated into the surrounding secular society, they often felt a need to cross the often insuperable and invisible boundary between the majority group and their own minority status, not knowing quite where they belonged. This made them, and other converts like them, what Lewin (1948) called "marginal men," and created a social psychological phenomenon in which personal self-doubts became characterized by Jewish self-hatred. Purporting to be "completed" Jews, today's "Messianic Jews" or "Jews for Jesus" reject other Jews for not accepting Jesus as the Messiah. They apparently believe themselves to be more acceptable to Christians than "ordinary" Jews, and do not see the fundamental incompatibility of claiming to be Jews while accepting Jesus as more than a teacher (Gittlesohn, 1979, pp.41-45). Lipson (1980) asserts that the peculiar syncretism observable in the Jews for Jesus movement uses ritual in an attempt to

> link the individual to a community of significant others through expression of what is important to the group. This function of what is of special significance to individuals who face a potential identity dilemma because they belong to a group that is socially marginal. While Hebrew Christians assert their dual orientation, rather than assimilating into Christian churches or keeping their beliefs secret from other Jews, they are accepted fully by neither Christians nor Jews (1980, pp.106-107).

Adoption of a faith more in common with that of the majority is perceived by the Christianized Jews as opening new doors of opportunity that had been closed to Jews (despite the anti-discrimination legislation of recent years). Yet many of these young people, alienated from and scornful of Jews in general, continue to be repelled by the residual Jewishness in themselves (Keniston, 1965; Loewenstein, 1951). In the contemporary Diaspora, the Jew who is so frustrated by barriers to his entry to the majority group and its perceived privileges often turns the resulting aggression not against the rejecting hostile and powerful Gentile majority, but against his own group. In a classic example of "blame the victim," he blames his failure to "gain acceptance in the majority on the behavior of a section of the Jewish group" (Herman, 1977, p.183). An example of this was seen earlier in our history in the reluctance of nineteenth-century assimilated German-Jewish immigrants to be identified with the poorer, cruder, more demonstrative Eastern European Jews who migrated to the United States at the beginning of the twentieth century (Evans, 1973). This was also true in England and especially France (Hyman, 1979). Indeed, from a psychoanalytic viewpoint, these and other Jewish anti-semites have identified with the aggressor (Loewenstein, 1951, p.144).

This "identification with the aggressor" lies at the heart of Jewish self-hatred and Jewish anti-semitism. Prepared to conform at almost any cost in his quest for acceptance and security, the Jewish anti-semite

> begins with appeasement and ends with imitation. He finds his Jewishness intolerable because it is at best a useless anachronism, excess baggage which impedes his progress in a Gentile world.... Like every other neurotic, the Jewish anti-semite feels that he can solve his difficulty only by ceasing to be himself, by concealing his identity from himself as well as from the outside world — or by running away. Whoever accepts in his heart the status of outcast in the Western world — be he assimilationist or anti-assimilationist — is a Jewish anti-semite (Pelcovitz, 1947, p.121).

From this point of view, the Jew who converts to another religion is running away from himself and his people rather than primarily committing himself to the new group. This is regressive conversion.

Another type of regressive conversion occurs when the hatred is directed not against oneself or one's group, but against one's parents, particularly the father or a father-figure. To some, conversions may be the resolution of an overextended Oedipal conflict in which the individual finds and accepts a welcoming and authoritative father-figure. Allison (1969), for instance, saw the conversion experience as an effort "to curtail sharply and also to realize and gratify an intense longing to fuse with the maternal figure in an undifferentiated matrix..., [an] internal representation of a strong and principled father [who] serves a crucial role in helping to counteract the yearning to retain the fusion with the mother, in aiding differentiation and separation, and in providing the basis for a coherent masculine identification" (p.24).

Given the psychological and existential questions and doubts of adolescence and young adulthood, Weininger suggests that in an ill-adjusted individual with "an intensely inquiring mind, a mounting anxiety leading to despair, an abandonment of striving will power, and acceptance by a good father figure, we have the soil upon which religious conversions take place" (1955, p.36). The inner struggle that ensues, especially the conflict with the father or authority symbol, may create such overwhelming anxiety and feelings of guilt that again the withdrawal or flight defense leads to the conversion experience (Salzman, 1953). The opposite extreme may also obtain where there is no conflict between family members because there is an unusually weak relationship between father and child (Schwartz & Kaslow, 1979). Here, the unconscious wish seems to be the childhood one for a protector, and the protector may be personified as Jesus, Reverend Moon, or a guru.

Most of the studies of converts or "born-again" Christians have had male subjects. This makes one wonder whether the theories seeking to explain such experiences are then only applicable to males. Are there differences in the group to which an individual converts depending upon one's gender or upon the type of parental figure being sought? For example, do those seeking a strong authoritarian figure tend to be more Jesus-oriented than Mary-oriented? Do they tend to become enmeshed in authoritarian cults more frequently than in less-structured faiths? Do they move to more orthodox, therefore more proscriptive, forms of their own original religion (e.g., orthodox or Chassidic Judaism)? Or, do those seeking a warm and nurturant maternal figure turn to the Roman Catholic Church with particular allegiance to Mary? Some clues may be found in the chapters to come that deal with voluntary converts and converts to cults.

There are two other categories of conversion. In one, the conversion is involuntary, either being seen as an alternative to execution as in the case of the Marranos during the Inquisition (Roth, 1947), or as the result of indoctrination during childhood without the consent of the child and/or the child's parents. Several instances of the latter category will be discussed in Part Two, ranging from the Mortara case of 1858 to the Finaly case that followed World War II. An example of this latter type of situation that was too common in the nineteenth century occurred in England in 1810, where the London Society for the Promotion of Christianity among the Jews, a Protestant missionary group,

> picked up a hungry fifteen-year-old boy, provided him with food and clothing, and persuaded him to defect from Judaism and accept baptism in the Anglican faith. When his father and mother discovered where he was and pleaded to be allowed to see him, the directors of the mission refused their request point-blank, fearing that the adolescent might be induced to recant and revert to Judaism. The Jewish community appealed to the King's Bench for the return of the youngster to his parents. The court, the London Society's historian reported with obvious satisfaction, rejected the Jewish petition after hearing the defense contend that since Judaism itself regards thirteen, the bar-mitzvah age, as the end of boyhood and the beginning of manhood, the parents could no longer be considered their son's legal guardian (Pollak, 1980, p.148).

38

The isolation and manipulation practiced in this case, not to mention the distorted reasoning entwined with a philosophy that the ends justified the means, were characteristic of most of the hundreds of documented accounts of the conversion of Jewish youth in the last and present centuries.

The circumstances in the seven cases of children included in Part Two range from kidnapping to overzealous proselytization, and caused varying degrees of consternation in the Church, within national governments, and in the Jewish communities around the world. The fear of the proselytizing agent that the youth would recant the conversion, as cited above, was typical also in these seven cases (and others). This, of course, raises the question of the depth of commitment to the new faith in instances of involuntary or manipulated conversion.

The other remaining category of conversion involves religious intermarriage. Although conversion undertaken to please the marital partner is frowned upon as the sole reason for such an action by Catholic and Jewish clergy alike, marriage is frequently the stimulus to religious conversion. In some instances, it is a *pro forma* conversion; that is, compliance without commitment. Often this decision is made to reduce the possibility of conflict between the spouses or in the parent-child relationship. In Gordon's study, most of his 45 subjects "stated that their thoughts turned in the direction of ecclesiastical conversion at the time when they determined to marry a person of another and different faith. Such conversions appear to have little or nothing to do with the inner struggle away from sin, evil, penitence, or even the striving after righteousness" (1967, p.4).

In other cases of intermarriage, there is a total commitment to the partner's faith after religious instruction. According to Lazerwitz (1971), converts in this instance had probably had less religious instruction in, and were more marginally attached to, their childhood faith than others in their original faith. He also avers that sincere converts tend to blend successfully into their new religious-ethnic community and to become more active religiously and organizationally than members native-born to it (1971, p.50). In both cases of conversion related to marriage, the conversion is voluntary, even where the choice is conversion or no marriage, and is based on informed consent.

Whatever the motivation for voluntary conversion, be it intellectual, regressive, or *pro forma*, there is a point in time when the decision is consciously made and appropriate steps are taken — that is, the ritual conversion takes place. Only in the sudden conversion experiences of this group might there be some doubt as to the convert's total awareness of making a choice. The question of voluntary informed choice will be raised in Part Two in connection with conversion to modern-day cults, an allegedly voluntary act, as well as the case of Alphonse Ratisbonne.

Looking ahead

Part Two of this study presents a number of case studies selected to illustrate the theme of proselytization, conversion, and commitment on a microscopic level. Four cases involve the involuntary conversion of Jewish children. The Bluth and Linneweil cases demonstrate the effects of manipulation under conditions of isolation. The studies of Theodore and Alphonse Ratisbonne examine the background of their conversions relevant to theoretical views, and illustrate the outcome of intense proselytization efforts. Finally, the modern cults are discussed, as they represent an amalgamation of the techniques of isolation, manipulation, and proselytization.

The third and final part of this work, "macroscopic" in scope, is concerned with the psychological effects of conversion of the individual, his or her family, and the Jewish community. Particular attention is paid to the nature and magnitude of the community responses to conversion efforts in general and the cases included here specifically. Comments on the practice of proselytization conclude the book.

CHAPTER II — CHILD AND ADOLESCENT CONVERSIONS

Proselytization

Throughout the history of mankind, we have seen conquerors attempt to impose the values of their culture on the vanquished, and majorities attempt to convert minorities to their beliefs or mores. This concept was especially applicable to Christianity, for a vital part of its belief was the necessity of bringing its message to all, based on the words of Jesus Christ: "Go therefore and make disciples of all nations" (Matthew 28:19). In response to such teaching, missionaries of nearly all Christian denominations performed their duty in the past and present either by aggressively seeking converts or by preaching the Christian message through social action [*Time*, 120, (26), 27 Dec. 1982].

As mentioned earlier, the United States and Western Europe began a continuing process of rapid change caused by modernization. Industrialization initiated the development of railroads, innovations in banking and commerce, mining and manufacturing. These changes affected, in turn, the relationship between the social classes, led to the growth of cities, and increasingly opened new avenues of opportunity for women and young people. Intellectual currents were also stimulated by the continuing economic prosperity and growth. There was increased respect for science and technology and a renewal of interest in education. However, modernization, while raising the standard of living, increasing technological progress, and stimulating worldliness also created anomie, alienation, apprehension, and often nostalgia for traditional values.

Churches, too, were challenged by these new forces as the secular spirit attentuated religious observances and participation. Various societies responded to the decline of traditional practices and institutions in different ways. In the United States, a plethora of evangelical, fundamentalist, and millenarian sects flourished; and some, such as the Mormons, the Seventh Day Adventists, Jehovah's Witnesses, actually became a part of mainstream American religion.

In France, on the other hand, there was little enthusiasm for new sects or cults, or for millenarian movements; rather a growth of innumerable miracle devotions and prophetic movements arose, of which the most illustrious was Lourdes (Harrison, 1979; Kselman, 1983, pp.84-103). The expression of religiosity was acknowledged by a widespread devotion to the Sacred Heart of Jesus, and even more intensely to the cult of Mary (Dansette, 1961, I, p.320). Almost spontaneously, a number of visions of Mary were widely reported. Often the apparitions were also accompanied by prophecies and warnings. The popularity of these manifestations was attested to by the frequency of pilgrimages to the sites of the reported miracles, and by the large amount of Marian devotion produced in art and iconography. Churches were dedicated to Mary, and confraternities such as the Association of the Living Rosary, the Children of Mary, and Our Lady of Victories were dedicated to her service. Besides the widespread devotion to Mary, there developed an effort by the Church missions to

reconvert lapsed or secular Catholics and to "save"
Protestants and Jews.

In England, evangelical movements were predominant.
One of the most prominent was the organized program to
convert Jews. It involved huge sums of money and unusual
expenditure of energy (most unsuccessfully). The most
famous of the missionary groups was the London Society for
the Promotion of Christianity Among the Jews which was
established in 1809 and still exists (Scult, 1973). These
missionaries not only sought converts in England, but also
established stations throughout Europe, the Middle East, the
United States, Asia, and Africa. Their techniques were based
on using social help, such as educating Jewish children,
giving money or jobs to possible converts, establishing
hospital clinics, through which they passed out their tracts
(Gidney, 1908).

Now, the attitude among some contemporary
mainstream Christian leaders questions the wisdom of active
concerted proselytization. Instead, they support the need to
gain the respect and acquisition of belief through example
and emulation. They especially deny either the wisdom or
the morality of a special "Mission to the Jews." They cite in
refutation the prejudice and persecution endured by Jews at
Christian hands. Many others, reacting to the horrors of
Auschwitz, feel morally unclean and unfit to preach to Jews
(Eckardt, 1967; Flannery, 1965; Ruether, 1974). In the State of
Israel, active government opposition to such Christian
activity abetted the doubts as to either the spiritual or
righteous wisdom of such active proselytization.

That, however, has not been the case in the past nor is it applicable to other present day denominations, especially "Jews for Jesus" or "Messianic Jews." Indeed, in the past, missions, especially those directed toward Jews, were fanatical and frequently overly zealous. Further, they were supported wholeheartedly by their congregations. Although their activities were conducted in good faith, their methods were often dubious, crass, and insensitive. Unfortunately, these methods, no longer countenanced by most Christians, are still used in a more refined manner by today's fringe sects and some esoteric cults.

The traditional Christian approach was that all men were sinners and only through faith in Jesus Christ could grace be granted. God speaks to all mankind. They further insisted that the church had a special task to appeal to Jews and to teach them the Gospel, for they claimed that the Gospel is the fulfillment of Judaism. Convinced of their moral superiority and constrained to "save" souls, missionaries behaved almost outrageously and, sometimes, without any thought of the social and emotional consequences of their deeds.

In Rome, the Pope required the compulsory attendance of 50 Jews and 50 Jewesses every Saturday afternoon at the Church of San Angelo in Pesheria. There a priest remonstrated with them on "their obstinacy, impertinence, and unbelief!" (Gidney, 1908, p.359).

The literature of the nineteenth century abounded with complaints of the abuses and practices of these missions. Not only Jews, but Catholics and Protestants assailed bitterly the efforts of missionaries to convert. The Jewish press expostulated over various attempts of the conversionists:

"They prey upon the young and poor who are invited to a comfortable snug room having lots of pictures upon the wall. They are given a nice tea with cakes ..." (*London Jewish Chronicle*, 6 February 1857). A case of bribery was related in the account of a poor family who were given ten shillings a week when they submitted to baptism (Ibid., 13 May 1853). Countless other articles warned readers of the perfidy of missionaries, of their failures and of their financing (Ibid., 21 January, 8 July, 1853; 27 September, 3, 5 October, 1854; 30 January, 3 April, 21 August, 1857). The French Jewish press expressed the same anxieties in eloquent editorials (c.f. *Verité Israelite,* 1861; *Archives Israelites, Univers Israelite*, 1860-61). In addition, Jewish organizations related legitimate complaints to the government of these overzealous activities. The grievances involved the baptism of runaway children, deathbed conversions, and the involuntary conversion of children of convicted felons (AN F 19, 11031).

Protestants were also subjected to these religious practices by a Catholic majority. In addition, Protestants were more harried by local French authorities because **their** evangelical activities irritated the Catholics who resented their missions as much as the Jewish community did (RDDM, 1858; *Journal de Bruxelles*, 31 December 1860; *Le Monde*, 5 January 1861).

The local administrations, anxious to placate feelings, persecuted Protestant evangelicals as public nuisances or as suspected political subversives. Moreover, Catholics were distressed at what they considered dishonest propaganda such as the medical dispensaries in which Bibles and religious tracts were issued along with medicines and Protestant attempts to seduce vulnerable Catholic youth.

Religious Mania

In Holland, breaches of good taste on the part of English evangelists toward the Jews frequently led to open violence and rioting by the protesting Jews. Missionaries often invaded synagogues during religious services and preached to the congregation. A Protestant, Pastor M. Wolsey, on one such occasion, also distributed Bibles and religious tracts. The Jewish congregation, angered, forcibly evicted him from their house of worship.

One of Wolsey's colleagues, M. Schwartz (a converted Jew), bitterly protested the expulsion in his paper *L'Herault* on the 30 July, 1858, claiming that the Methodists acted in good faith and were doing God's work. The Jews had behaved badly, he asserted.

The Jewish congregation, already irritated by the missionaries, were even more annoyed by the tone of Schwartz's paper. One young boy, named Hirsh (fifteen years of age), became even more incensed and responded to the provocation by attacking and stabbing Schwartz in the chest several times. Fortunately, although severely wounded, the pastor recovered. Hirsh was immediately arrested and claimed that he had acted during a "black-out." The adolescent was found guilty of premeditated assault with a deadly weapon under extenuating circumstances of "religious mania." He was sentenced to twelve years' imprisonment (*Gazette d'Utrecht*, 12 August 1859).

What made the case so tragic was that young Hirsh's past conduct had been exemplary; his teachers thought that he was brilliant and would distinguish himself in his chosen future of medicine. However, he had become rigid in his religious beliefs and began to view the distribution of the evangelical propaganda as weapons which would destroy the religion of his fathers. One report commented that "... his sick imagination eventually resulted in a violent act which also destroyed his future." (*The Amsterdam Gazette* further said: "The distribution of pamphlets in synagogues is not reasonable, it is indecent!") This statement was made in spite of the fact that this paper and the Dutch press in general felt both respect and sympathy for the aims of the missionaries, and lauded them for their sacrifices and good faith. However, most also agreed that the act of Hirsh was the direct consequence of fanatical religiosity on the part of both the Jews and the Methodists. Cahen, in a French Jewish paper, summed up what may be the most succinct analysis of the affair: "The audacious provocation of missionaries had overexcited the imagination of a sick mind." He added that religion should not be marked by any violence whether in good faith or not; religious principles of others should not be attacked and not disputed. The preachers should only propose and not impose, and he ended his editorial deploring the excesses of missionaries in general (*Archives Israélites*, August 1858).

The Mortara Affair

Far more tragic even than the case of young Hirsh were the numerous incidents of involuntary conversion that occurred in Europe in the nineteenth century. Most involved the Catholic Church and the forced conversion of Jewish children, which illustrated the persistence of religious anti-semitism. Several cases involving the Catholic Church and the forced, or involuntary conversion of Jewish children were illustrative of these practices. The most famous and publicized incident was that of the kidnapping of Edgardo Mortara in the Papal States in 1858.

The Mortara Affair occurred in Bologna in the Papal States. These States had laws restricting the rights of Jews in their daily lives. One such law prohibited Jews from employing non-Jews (Catholics in particular). The Mortaras, however, employed a young Catholic female as a nursemaid, although whether in ignorance or disregard of the law is unknown. The maid secretly baptized one of their children, Edgardo, when he was ill and she thought he was dying. Subsequently, after she had revealed the episode to her confessor, Edgardo was forcibly removed from his family's care when he was six years old, and was taken to Rome by the Papal authorities.

This action was based on an interpretation of a canon law that stated that a child baptized in the Roman Catholic faith must be educated as a Christian. Although the Church forbade baptism of heretics or infidels against their will or baptism of their children against the parents' will, that ruling did not apply to a person who was dying. In the event of possible death, it became the duty of the Catholic to baptize the individual in order to save an expiring soul. With this guideline, it should come as no surprise that the Mortara case was not unusual. Jewish children were frequently abducted under this pretext for baptism and raised as Christians. The difference in 1858 was that the Jewish communities in Europe and the United States felt strong enough to protest the action in the case of Edgardo Mortara (Isser, 1981; Korn, 1958).

Young Edgardo was kept isolated from his family and other Jews in the House of Catechumens in Rome. Parental consternation and protest, diplomatic pressures (especially by Napoleon III), and outraged cries of Jewish groups in several countries were to no avail. When Sir Moses Montefiore, for example, protested the affair in 1859, he was told that Edgardo would be allowed to decide his own destiny at age 17 or 18 (Volli, 1960). Caen said of this comment by Cardinal Antonelli that it was a "mockery to good sense," for by then the boy would have had 12 years of exclusively Catholic education (Volli, 1960, p.36).

The Pope remained adamant in maintaining the separation of the child from his family. It was reported that Pius IX expressed his decision in these terms: "How would he, the head of the Church, answer the last solemn judgment if he sent back to Judaism a soul that freely sought the salvation of the Christian religion. He [Pius IX] regretted the occurrence deeply. He was well aware how the enemies of the Church would turn it to account, but he could not for that reason compromise with his conscience. . . . His decision was now unalterable. It was that the child should be educated in the Christian religion ... but that his parents should have access to him whenever they pleased" (Isser, 1981, p.70). The child was educated, trained, and inculcated with values different from those of his family. That he appeared to be thoroughly indoctrinated was revealed by the contemporary reports of the child's behavior. When interviewed after his abduction, he responded in rote sentences in a manner quite unnatural for his age (London Times, 20 October 1868).

Although the Papal authorities promised the Mortaras that they could visit their child, they were harried by the police, and Edgardo remained hidden away. Finally, the parents received permission to visit the boy, who then cried and shouted his desire to return home. Even more frustrated, the Mortaras left Rome, sold their business, abandoned their home in Bologna, and began a long, bitter, and fruitless struggle to recover their son (Volli, 1960). Subsequent reports clearly showed that the family unit was disrupted and the child himself was effectively estranged from his parents (Volli, 1960). The mother's health, too, was undermined by the tragedy of her loss (AN, MSS F 19, 1789, 10 October 1861).

Joseph Coen

Another kidnapping in Rome, which evoked almost the same kind of protest (although somewhat less vehement), occurred in 1864. The victim was an 11-year-old boy named Joseph Coen, who was apprenticed to a shoemaker. A customer, a priest, moved by the child's charm, was determined to save the boy's soul. Young Joseph delivered the priest's mended shoes to the rectory, and was received with kindness, plied with sweets, and enticed into taking a ride in the priest's carriage. Once inside, he was abducted and brought to the House of Catechumens, where he remained despite his tearful protests. Actions and appeals by the distraught parents and arguments by the Jewish communities were to no avail. The mother herself, driven by despair, went to the House of Catechumens where she cried and implored for the boy's return. Her screams so irritated the rector that he ordered the mother's arrest. She was finally released only after she was told to be silent and

agreed (Stampa, Italia, Nazione, and Diritto, reported in the
London *Jewish Chronicle*, 23 September 1864).

As in 1858 in the case of Edgardo Mortara, diplomatic
protests and public outcries from across Western Europe
could not and did not alter the Papal authorities' attitudes.
The child Joseph was duly baptized and separated from his
family. In despair, the family moved to Leghorn, where the
distraught mother was cared for by the Jewish community
(London *Jewish Chronicle*, 4 November 1864; AN F19, 1937,
Coen dossier).

Some months later, a Genevan pastor reported in a Swiss
paper that he had met Mme. Mortara and promised to visit
her son. "She showed us as much by the tears which filled
her eyes as by her words how sore is still the wound at her
heart" (**Bouquet Helvetique** cited in London *Jewish Chronicle*,
24 February 1865). After visiting the House of Catechumens,
the pastor reported that Edgardo Mortara was "assiduous in
his studies and that he was not oppressed." Furthermore,
both boys (Joseph Coen as well) were receiving an excellent
Catholic education. However, the minister did not see
Joseph Coen, though he later visited Joseph's mother who
had recovered from a nervous breakdown. "She was
restored now," he wrote, "but she weeps still" (Ibid.).

In both cases, the family unit was adversely affected, and
both boys were effectively estranged from their parents. By
adolescence, the young Mortara spoke of his voluntary and
firm commitment to the Church, an assertion made only after
being totally educated in an alien and restricted environment
during his formative years (Brown, 1977, p.249; Schwartz &
Isser, 1979). An unusually proficient student of languages,

he became a devoted priest. He moved to Poitiers, France, in 1870, where he died in 1940. He did have a meeting with his family as an adult, but received them coldly, insensitively, and without affection, as he plied them with exhortations to convert! (Volli, 1960). In contrast, Joseph Coen's final choices and fate remain unknown.

The Finaly brothers

Other kidnappings following the Second World War reflected excessive religious ardor and insensitive proselytization, and involved even greater conspiratorial efforts than these early cases. The Finaly brothers, Robert and Gerard, lived in Southern France. They were entrusted by their parents to the nursery run by nuns of the St.Vincent de Paul order shortly before the couple were arrested and killed in early 1944. The boys were then about 18 and 33 months old. They had both been circumcised, a point later emphasized to indicate that the parental intent had been to raise the boys as Jews. As risks increased in the area of the nursery, the children were moved — first to the convent of Notre Dame de Sion near Grenoble, and later to a municipal nursery in their home community, where the directress, Mlle. Brun, took them in defiance of Nazi laws. Both the local mayor and friends of the family knew and wrote (later) that the children were to be entrusted ultimately to an aunt, Mrs. Fischel, if the parents did not return from Nazi captivity.

After the war ended and the parents indeed did not return, Mlle. Brun became their guardian in November 1945 through the device of a legally-appointed "family council," which in this case had no family members on it. In 1948, she had the boys baptized to avoid their recovery by the surviving family. Moreover, the children had, all along, been exposed to Catholic doctrines in the nursery and at the local school.

Meanwhile, the family sued for recovery of the boys, also using the family council that had ultimately been appointed for their side. The court ordered Mlle. Brun to return the youngsters to an aunt, Mrs. Rosner, who lived in Israel, in late 1949. Mlle. Brun, defying the court order, enlisted the help of Franciscans, Dominicans, and nuns of Notre Dame de Sion in hiding the children in France and nearby countries. The court battles continued into the early 1950's, as the boys were secreted in parochial schools, convents, and monasteries in Spain (Keller, 1960). Higher church officials and the Pope himself in this case, reversed the position taken earlier by Pius IX in the Mortara affair. They agreed that the boys were to be returned to their aunt (Schwartz & Isser, 1981).

By June of 1953, the boys were returned to France in conformity with an agreement reached in March of that year between the opposing parties. The agreement stipulated, among other things, that "the children would remain free from pressure as to religion and, if brought to Israel (where their aunt, to whom the courts gave custody, now lived and who did take them there in July 1953) would receive a French education" (*America*, 11 July 1953, p.370). With that, the boys faded from public view.

It is now known what happened to the boys after their recovery by the family because *France-Soir* of 25 July 1978 published a retrospective article on the affair, including an interview with Robert Finaly, the older of the two brothers.

Then 37, he was a surgeon in Beersheba, a profession chosen because it was his father's. Gerard, a year younger, was a career officer in the Israeli army. Both men were married, and each had two children.

In the interview, Dr. Finaly said that Mlle. Brun and others who hid the brothers from 1948 to 1953 told them of the dire consequences if they were recovered by their family in Israel. These lies made him somewhat distrustful of people when he discovered their nature. Gerard, he said, did not develop the same trait.

Raised as Catholics by Mlle. Brun, a factor which saved their lives, the Finaly brothers had gone to mass upon arriving in Israel twenty-five years before. As they adapted to their new country, they gradually adopted Jewish beliefs and cultural values. Dr. Finaly indicated, however, that he did not consider himself an observant Jew, and attended services mainly at the High Holy Days.

Although grateful to Mlle. Brun for saving their lives, Dr. Finaly could not undestand her obstinacy in hiding himself and his brother and impeding their reunion with their relatives. He noted that other Catholics saved Jewish children without baptizing them or separating them from family any longer than necessary. Furthermore, said Dr. Finaly, fear of loss of affection could not have been Mlle. Brun's primary motive, since they were cared for principally by one of her assistants. Indeed, Dr. Finaly expressed the belief that had Mlle. Brun returned him and his brother to their family more readily, she would have been regarded affectionately as an "aunt" with exchanges of visits. Under the circumstances, however, he felt that a visit to her would not have been comfortable for either party.

Dr. Finaly concluded the interview by saying that, after all, the matter had all worked out for the best, so why dwell on the past. He certainly seemed aware of all that had transpired and of the consequence of the long custody battle, but attempted to balance his feelings of bitterness and gratitude when pressed to recall those early years. His adjustment appeared to be related to the change in environment in pre-adolescence and, doubtless, to gentle handling in the area of religion by the boys' very determined aunt and uncle (*France-Soir* , 1978).

Anneke Beekman

A similar case of betrayal of parental trust occurred in The Netherlands. Anneke Beekman, a baby, was given to some Dutch women for care when her parents were deported (and later killed by the Nazis). After the war, attempts were made to place the child in a Jewish family's home, but as in France, the protective but over-zealous Dutch ladies were determined to keep Anneke Catholic. She was hidden in various convents in Holland and Belgium. All attempts by the remnants of the Dutch Jewish community to recover the child, the cooperation of the courts, and wide use of media, were futile. Unlike the French situation, the Dutch Roman Catholic Church was not cooperative, and the Dutch Jews were too weak and powerless to achieve any success (Fishman, 1978).

In a television interview with an Israeli correspondent, the young woman, who had by this time come of age, freely admitted that she knew nothing about Judaism, nor did she have any realization of the significance of Auschwitz. She had married a Catholic Frenchman and remained oblivious to her past.

Saul Friedlander

Saul Friedlander, a contemporary scholar, related his early experience during the Second World War, which parallels the two previous cases up to a point, in autobiographical writings. As he related his trials in his memoirs, on 16 July 1942 his mother turned him over to a Catholic school, begging their protection of her young son until the end of the terrible war. In return for saving the boy, Saul's father agreed that his child would be raised a Catholic. The child at first resisted, running back to his family in his anxiety to remain with his parents, but they were firm. He was returned to the Catholic school where his name was changed, and he was educated and duly baptized into the Catholic faith. After bouts of melancholia and severe depression, he gradually adjusted to his new life and identity, quite repressing his earlier life, and became so devoted to his new identity that he seriously contemplated becoming a priest.

As in the Finaly and Beekman cases, the boy's parents never returned. Just as the war ended and Saul was to leave the school, the well-intentioned sisters sent him to visit a priest, hoping to protect him from baleful outside influences. As the boy spoke of his wish to become a Jesuit, the good priest responded by asking the boy, "Didn't your parents die at Auschwitz?" Saul was suddenly confronted with his forgotten past. As Friedlander explained it,

> The attitude of Father L. himself profoundly influenced me: to hear him speak of the lot of the Jews with so much emotion and respect must have been an important encouragement for me. He did not press me to choose one path or the other — and perhaps he would have preferred to see me remain Catholic — but his sense of justice (or was it a profound charity?) led him to recognize my right to judge for myself by helping me to renew the contact with my past (Friedlander, 1979a, p.57).

Friedlander left the Catholic environment, resumed his former name, went to Israel, and eventually became a scholar. His point was that he was given a choice, as the others had not been given, and he consciously elected to resume his Jewish identity (Friedlander, 1979b). His experience provided a contrast to that of the earlier cases where those children had been deprived of any choice, or as in the Finaly case, acquired a choice only through legal action.

Involuntary Conversion

In most of the outcomes of missionary efforts cited above, the salient factor was that these were young children involuntarily converted and separated forcibly or by circumstances from their parents. There is, however, little evidence in the psychological literature that is applicable to these affairs. For example, the usual studies of the effects of foster home placement and institutionalization are not applicable here. The literature on separation anxiety deals principally with quite young children, mostly preschoolers, and is only tangentially relevant since the primary issue is not the quality of institutional care, or, indeed, separation anxiety itself. The few papers written on kidnapping are concerned with contemporary political kidnappings (mostly of adults), or with those kidnappings in which the victim was killed, as in the Lindbergh case.

There are few studies, if any, available on the effects of kidnapping on children or their families, or on ideological conversion of the young. In both the Mortara and Coen affairs, these factors were pertinent. To evaluate the effects of the events, we must draw upon the contemporary social sciences of psychology and sociology to provide illumination.

In the case of kidnapping, Hentig has pointed out that "The young are easy victims not only because they are physically undeveloped, but [also] because they are immature in moral personality and moral resistance" (Hentig, 1948; c.f. Freud & Burlingham, 1943; Hall, 1904; Meerloo, 1956; Schafer, 1974). It is not surprising then that the young Edgardo Mortara, abducted at age six, or even Anneke Beekman, were effectively converted to Catholicism, with Mortara becoming a canon of the Church and a professor of theology as an adult.

In all of the cases examined here, there were certain common elements that contributed to the involuntary conversion. Each of the children was isolated from family and normal social supports. Each was isolated from contrary input. Certainly each child was vulnerable. And each was indoctrinated on a full-time basis with a new ideology, conformity to which was reinforced with resulting extinction of former beliefs. Only in the Friedlander case, due to the fortuitous meeting with Father L., was there true freedom of choice.

It is not only the story of involuntary conversions of children that is told here, however, but also that of those who, for good or ultimately malevolent purposes, raised these children. In the Mortara and Coen cases, there was an intransigent Church that believed its rights superseded familial and civil rights. In the modern wartime cases, where trust had been placed in the ability of Catholics to hide Jewish children successfully, that trust was abused when the need for protection was past in both the Finaly and Beekman cases.

In Friedlander, on the other hand, the priest made no attempt to keep the boy, or to assert that, having been baptized, he must now remain a Catholic. Similarly, in Le Chambon, a village in Southern France, the Protestant minister who guided the mission of saving Jewish refugees made no effort to convert them (Hallie, 1980).

Not all children reacted to the wartime isolation and distress in the same way. One boy rescued by a priest **adamantly** resisted all attempts at his conversion. He recalled that "I refuse to attend mass; the priest punishes me; I stand my ground ..." (Vegh, 1984, p.152). Others, frightened and isolated, turned instead to the comfort of the Church and copied the behavior of their friends and rescuers (Weinstein, 1985). "The Church," related one woman, became my refuge. "I began to pray for my parents to come back as soon as possible. It never crossed my mind that they wouldn't come back. ... But I promised God that if they came back soon, I would convert. Had they come back, I should no doubt have become a fervent Catholic!" (Vegh, 1984, p.126)

All of those who hid Jews, adults or children, disobeyed the laws of the Nazi Occupation forces and took great risks in being defiant. That there were different responses to this risk foreshadows the varying responses we perceive today with respect to conversions of young people that similarly raise questions about the level of informed choice and voluntary action involved.

Manipulative practices of well meaning missionaries were frequently directed to the young. Intuitively exploiting fear and guilt through isolation and persuasion, missionaries were able to convert adolescents and young adults. The psychological factors enabling them to achieve their ends were the social relationships, the desire to conform to the majority, or the achievement of peer approval. So important was this motive, especially among adolescents, that missionaries frequently utilized social networks and other peer group mechanisms to aid in proselytization. Peer pressures became more effective in reinforcing receptivity to proselytization if the individual was vulnerable, a state that psychologists characterize as occurring in an individual who is emotionally labile and who is placed in a position where he/she feels inadequate, lonely, and insecure. Temporary failures can cause such periods of loss of self esteem and nagging doubts of self-worth. Such feelings have at one time or another affected all of us, but the condition is more prevalent among adolescents and young adults, who have more difficulty ameliorating or solving their anxieties. When feeling vulnerable, the individual may react by resorting to impulsive, dependent, or irresponsible behavior. It is at such moments that the individual is vulnerable and is most prone, under the proper circumstances, to alter his normal responses and actions, including the possibility of conversion to another set of beliefs.

Some adolescents and young adults making the transition to maturity and independence do so with a minimum of struggle. They meet the expectations and demands of their community and fulfill the responsibilities with little fuss. In changing societies, however, those transitions become more difficult and young people tend to become more confused, rebellious, and unable to effect independence. Their behavior can be characterized by a variety of forms of deviant behavior, varying somewhat with the times in which they live. In our own time, they have turned to alcoholism, drug addiction, suicide, and "dropping out." They may also respond to this period of crisis by seeking to undermine established authority, by revolutionary activity, or by subverting the religious establishment which they perceive as hypocritical and self-serving. Often this kind of rebellion is also characterized by a conversion to a faith very different from one's own or a search for an alternative situation in which one can flee from freedom and maturity (Ostow, 1980).

The examples to be cited next here are those of young people who were particularly vulnerable to the blandishment of the proselytizer, or those who found the road to full adulthood so painful that conversion offered an alternative form of rebellion and service. All occurred in nineteenth century France in an atmosphere very different from that of Rome of the 1850's or our own time. The Napoleonic Code, the French law, provided that parental civil rights superseded those of the church, and it guaranteed religious freedom which permitted Jews to practice their religion openly. (Note: This does not mean that attempts at proselytization did not occur or that anti-semitism did not exist. They did in the nineteenth century as they do today in France.)

The first of these cases, entitled "the Mallet Affair," involved cases of involuntary conversion. The "Affair" began in 1853 and came to public notice in 1861, only three years after the kidnapping of young Mortara. The episode's origins in 1853 occurred when Anna Bluth, aged twenty-two years, came as a young teacher to Paris from her native Prussia, seeking a teaching position.

Anna was alone, separated from a very large family, and she knew few people in France. In a strange environment, she felt especially isolated and insecure. It was at this moment of vulnerability that she met Abbé Theodore Ratisbonne, a former Jew who had himself converted to Catholicism (c.f. Ch.III). He was an unusually silver-tongued and dynamic personality, a brilliant preacher who was especially effective with women. Anna, as had many before her, succumbed to Ratisbonne's impassioned blandishments, and was subsequently converted to the Catholic Church. She became an ardent and dedicated believer, desirous of proving her allegiance by seeking the conversion of her own family, an attitude common to many converts (Lofland, 1966). Further, she completed the identity alteration by abandoning her old name at her baptism, selecting the name Maria Siona as her new name.

Anna's father, Jacob Bluth, was a struggling Hebrew teacher, married to Sarah Levy, and with eight children requiring support. The children were Anna (the eldest), Minchen, Adolph, Louis, Louise, Sophie, Isadore, and Elisabeth. When Anna requested that Minchen stay with her in Paris, the parents readily assented. Minchen, then seventeen years old and under her sister's influence while separated from the rest of the family, was easily persuaded to convert also. She took the name Gabrielle. She was given a shop to manage by her patrons where she earned an adequate salary and, of course, became indebted to them.

When Jacob Bluth came to Paris to visit with his daughters, Anna prevailed upon him to stay with Abbé Ratisbonne. The evidence available suggests that Jacob was a weak, vacillating, insecure individual. In the eight days that he stayed with the Abbé, he was duly converted, too, through the eloquence and warmth of his host, although Ratisbonne was skeptical of Jacob's depth of commitment and enthusiasm (Isser, 1979). Once Jacob accepted the new religion, he could no longer teach Hebrew in his native Weimar or in Prussia. Therefore he remained in Paris giving German lessons, and he, too, became dependent on the generosity of his Catholic patrons. Responding to the pressure of his oldest daughter and Ratisbonne, he then sent for the rest of his family. He managed to convert and have his three little girls, Louise, Sophie, and Elisabeth, baptized, but his wife Sarah held fast to her ancestral faith and was determined to keep the other children Jewish as well. She therefore fled to London with the younger children and received aid from the English Jewish community.

Meanwhile, Maria Siona (Anna) took a better teaching position in the city of Cambrai, Department of the Nord, where she became acquainted with the Canon of the Cathedral, an Abbé Mallet. She brought her brother Adolph with her, apparently despite their mother's opposition, and he, too, was converted and worked in Cambrai as a professor in the local college. All members of the family who had been converted were also economically aided by their proselytizers, and were, because of this dependence, the more responsive to their suggestions.

As new converts, zealous to prove their loyalty, both Adolph and Anna were determined to secure the conversion of their siblings. They convinced their father to reassert his patriarchal rights, a feat which brought him the return of Sarah and the younger children. The entire family was reunited at Cambrai. The three younger daughters, Louise, Sophie, and Elisabeth, were sent to Paris to be educated free of charge in the school of the Convent of Notre Dame de Sion (founded by Abbé Ratisbonne). The boys were sent to other Catholic schools.

Soon, however, the Bluth parents, much to their distress, discovered that their daughter Anna (Maria Siona) had become the mistress of the Canon Mallet, and that further, when the younger girls had spent their vacation in Cambrai, Mallet's behavior toward them had been much too bold and licentious. Dismayed, the Bluths, accompanied by Adolph, returned to Paris. There, Jacob and his son abjured their conversion and re-embraced Judaism. At this point, the parents requested that their children be returned to them from the Catholic schools. The boys were sent home without incident, but the girls were not. Louise, Sophie, and

Elisabeth were instead kidnapped by Canon Mallet and deliberately secreted from their family by various religious authorities. The elder Bluths then sought to locate and recover their daughters with the help of the French government.

For two-and-a-half years, Louise was hidden under false names in the convents of the Sainte-Union Order in Belgium and France so that her parents could not find her. Frightened by tales of impending spiritual doom if she returned home, she cooperated in this plan. Finally, when she came of age, she resisted further exhortations that she become a nun and she returned to her parents.

Elisabeth, too, was hidden by her sister Anna (Maria Siona), with the help of several ecclesiastics and was transported from one convent to another, five or six in all, of the Sainte-Union congregations in France and Belgium, all under assumed names. Abbé Mallet was again largely instrumental in hiding and transporting the young girl. She was also subjected to massive and intensive indoctrination. Because she was younger, more malleable, but more emotionally dependent upon her mother, she reacted to the separation and ideology manipulation badly. Soon Elisabeth began to suffer from hallucinations and periods of religious exaltations. She became so deranged that the Mother Superior of the Mother House at Douai petitioned the prefect to admit Elisabeth, by now in her mid-teens, to the mental hospital at Lille. The government authorities, who had energetically tried to find the children, notified her family, but the girl was already hopelessly insane.

The third sister, Sophie, also kidnapped and hidden in various convents, disappeared completely. The government persisted in its search and finally located her, almost a year after the others were found. She had been placed in a convent of the Sisters of Sainte-Union located near London. Her name had been changed, and, equally indoctrinated, she had assumed a new identity and had begun preparations to become a nun. She refused contact with her family, and was especially scornful of her mother.

To make the situation even more tragic, Maria Siona also became deranged, as the result either of guilt or, as rumored, of an abortion. The French government, disturbed by the kidnappings and their outcomes and what it considered excessive proselytization, arrested and tried Abbé Mallet for the crime of kidnapping minors. He was found guilty and sentenced to six years in prison. The Mother House of the Convent of Sainte-Union was suppressed for its role in the abductions, despite the stormy protest of the Archbishop of Cambrai (Isser, 1979). The damage to the Bluth family, however, was irreparable.

Vulnerability

The Linneweil Affair was another conversion event that erupted shortly after the Mallet Affair, although it has a less important role in history. Nevertheless, it provides an insightful case study of adolescent vulnerability and proselytization, well-documented because Elisabeth Linneweil herself described the ordeal in great detail and almost as the situation occurred. This episode took place in the Department of Haut Marne in the city of Riom in Southeastern France (A.D. Haut-Loire, Riom MSS).

Elisabeth Linneweil was born in 1843 in Puy de Dome, in the neighborhood of the city of Clermont, the daughter of an itinerant Jewish peddler and his mistress. The Linneweils were very poor and had no permanent home, as their business necessitated constant travel. The couple, therefore, left the infant with a wet nurse who was paid for six months' care in advance, a practice that was still common in mid-nineteenth century France. The father promised to pay all additional expenses that might be incurred. Depite all his good intentions, however, he was unable to meet all of the necessary financial obligations of his infant daughter. The wet nurse thereupon went to Clermont and left the child at a hospice. In response to the request of the civil authorities, the Jewish community assumed responsibility for the child and subsidized the cost of her care. The leaders of the Jewish community located a childless elderly couple named Estener to assume the care of the baby. The Esteners became her foster parents, treating her as if she were their own child, and even renamed her, giving her the name of Sarah Estener. Although they loved her as doting parents, they did remain in touch with the Linneweils, informing them of their daughter's development and growth (A.D. MSS). The evidence indicated that she was a sweet, obedient child who achieved high grades in school (Ibid.).

As Sarah (Elisabeth) moved into her adolescent years, her foster parents became ill, and their friends, a neighboring Catholic couple named Collat, took care of the young girl. When the Esteners died, the Collats became the executors of their estate, and at the same time offered Sarah the shelter of their home. Learning of the death of the Esteners, Meyer Linneweil sought to reclaim his daughter and expressed the desire to bring her to himself. Lacking funds, economic

necessity forced him to sell goods along the way, delaying a
speedy trip to Clermont and Riom. However, once he
arrived in Riom and tried to contact his daughter, he found
that she had suddenly and inexplicably disappeared. The
distraught father contacted the local officials of the Ministry
of Justice who uncovered a plot to separate the girl per-
manently from her real parents. She was secreted, like the
Bluth girls, in a variety of religious establishments —
nunneries and schools — under several pseudonyms, while
efforts were made to convert her to Catholicism (A.D., Acte
d'Accusation).

Elisabeth had cooperated with the Collats and their
friends because she believed their tales that her father had
abandoned her, and then later "sold" her. They convinced
her that, if she returned to him, he would strip her of the
inheritance she had from the Esteners, and leave her to die
before she came of age (*Archives Israelite*,. November 1861).
At this point, Elisabeth was especially vulnerable. She was
seventeen when her foster parents died, and she did not
know or remember her real parents. She felt isolated and
frightened, and was totally dependent upon the Collats for
affection and security. Furthermore, she had, from her
infancy, suffered maternal deprivation, a common
occurrence in those days, which was reflected in her passive
and dependent personality and an excessive desire to please
(Bowlby, 1958). These traits were reinforced further by her
status as a foster child, of which she was quite aware. At the
same time, the foster home had provided her with a highly
satisfactory emotional experience, reinforced by the
additional affection of her foster parents' friends and
associates, the Collats. The death of the Esteners came as a
second cruel instance of parental deprivation. Moreover, the

death of her elderly foster parents not only renewed her sense of being abandoned, but aroused the adolescent fear of death itself. As we know from modern research, bereavement is a painful experience for most people, but tends to have its greatest impact on the young (Miller, 1971; Silverman & Silverman, 1970; Simos, 1979).

Elisabeth's desire to convert to Catholicism did not stem from basic unhappiness, absence of direction or goals, oedipal conflicts, or other psychopathology or maladaptation. She represented, instead, the case of an insecure and thoroughly dependent individual caught in a moment of decision, faced with fears of the unknown — meeting and living with parents who she did not know. This fear of the unknown, anxiety about the future, is a natural concomitant of personality development. The fear of confronting parents, the fear of being rejected (again), the fear of the unknown, the fear of new relationships, and the fear of being alone — all of these are natural sources of anxiety for the most normal and sensitive young person (Fromm, 1950; Maslow, 1954; Spero, 1977). In Elisabeth's case, her fears made her even more vulnerable to the proselytization and suggestions of her protectors, the Collats.

Two priests who interviewed Elisabeth during this period refused to baptize her. Their denials were based upon the precedent of past scandals, but they noted further that a baptism would prevent an eventual reconciliation between father and daughter, leading to a repudiation of parental authority (AD, deposition of Father Rouisson). Elisabeth's sincerity in requesting baptism was never doubted by her interlocutors, but they were aware from her conversation that much of her interest in Catholicism was bound to her affection for the Collats rather than her own intensive longing for a religious commitment (AD, deposition of Father Rouisson).

Ultimately, despite every attempt to hide the young woman and baptize her, the police finally located Elisabeth and she was returned to her parents. Reconciled with her father, mother, and an uncle, she discovered that her former protectors had lied to her. "I have learned to know and love my family who cherish me also" (*Archives Israelite*, November 1861; Isser, 1984), she wrote. The Collats and Pauline Legay, a friend and co-conspirator, were indicted and tried for the crime of kidnapping. They were exonerated of the criminal charges by a legal technicality (the Linneweils were not legally married, so family rights had not been violated), but they were declared guilty on civil grounds of injuring the plaintiffs, the Linneweil family, and were fined 3000 francs (A.D., Memoire).

An Analysis

These cases suggest that in the past, as well as in the present era, adolescents can prove especially quick to respond to missionary activity under suitable environmental circumstances. Maria Siona, Elisabeth Linneweil, and other Jewish youngsters during World War II such as Saul Friedlander, were susceptible to such efforts, as are many young people on our college campuses or those who are frightened and "runaways."

The need to secure approval and continuing support of the Collats and their friends led Elisabeth to demand baptism

and agree to the flight from her family. As we have seen,
Jewish children during the Holocaust years were even more
vulnerable to the pressures of their teachers and local
communities because of similar dependence upon them.
Deprived of their parents, communal associations, all
familiar and loving relationships, they, too, were totally
dependent upon their pro tem guardians for emotional and
physical security. Obviously, under these circumstances,
and often without comprehending fully what they were
doing, many children accepted baptism (Friedlander, 1979b).
The devout, in some cases, were willing to take advantage of
these young people — as in the cases of both the Bluth girls
and Elisabeth — and in a misguided urge to "save souls,"
were often able to convince the naive to follow their orders,
to evade the law, and to reject their heritage and their family.
They were also willing to practice deception, using
falsehoods to discredit the motives of the families of origin
and communities. In the Finaly case, the boys were
convinced that they would be placed in an orphanage;
Elisabeth had been told she was not wanted except for her
inheritance; Anneke Beekman was never informed of her
background at all. In at least two instances, the young
people were embittered afterward when they learned of
these cruel calumnies.

On the other hand, individual members of the clergy
differed in their attitudes toward such proselytization of
vulnerable young children and adolescents. In the Linneweil
case, while many priests and nuns cooperated in hiding her,
there were others who were more sensitive to the family
relationships and emotional bonds. Similarly, after World
War II, many clergy exhibited compassion for Jewish
suffering and the survivors. As we have seen, Saul

Friedlander related such an episode in his memoirs, and in the furor over the Finaly kidnapping, the Church officially supported the boys' aunt.

Since children and adolescents are often emotionally fragile and insecure, they desperately desire to "belong," to be accepted, and they seek a sense of community. The normal developmental need to derive a system of belief and values that involves commitment and the human need to have a sense of belonging are critical factors that are manipulated in cases such as those just discussed. If responsible adults, such as Jacob Bluth, cannot provide satisfactory social bonding, the young person often seeks satisfaction in the approval of other adults — Abbé Ratisbonne and the Collats, for instance — or those of their own age group (Stark & Bainbridge, 1980). As we examine the cases of Abbé Ratisbonne himself, and that of his younger brother, in the next chapter, this point is made again, although in different ways than with the younger subjects of study.

CHAPTER III — ADULT CONVERSIONS

Proselytization, frequently a key component of conversion, is varied in its intensity, techniques, and honesty. Overzealous, insensitive approaches were used by missionaries in the past, as we have seen, and are still used today. However, intensive, callous, and/or devious evangelistic efforts have often been less successful than more direct, sincere, and honest persuasion, especially where environmental and emotional forces already provide a background conducive to change. The pervasive secularization of society in the nineteenth century, abetted by rapid industrialization and the even swifter pace of innovation, provided for the effective weakening of traditional values and social bonding. Such weakening was manifested by increases in religious intermarriage, desires for social mobility and economic advancement, all of which became strong motives for conversion to the faith of the majority. An example can be seen in post-Revolutionary France.

The combination of the Enlightenment and the emancipation of Jews during the French Revolution freed them from the ghetto and gave them choices about entering the modern world. The result was rapid assimilation of Jews into the mainstream culture in France and also in England and Germany, where a more secular culture was widespread. Many young people, as is true even today, recoiled from actual conversion because of a personal sense of honor and loyalty to family and community. Instead, they became deists or agnostics and simply refrained from active religious observance. Others, long alienated from Judaism, finally converted openly after prolonged estrangement from or the death of their parents. One such case in the eighteenth century was that of the famous intellectual Rachel Varnhagen (Arendt, 1960), but there were many others like her (Mahler, 1971).

In France specifically, though small in actual numbers, so many converts came from among the brightest, young, intellectual, well-to-do Jews that the Jewish community expressed consternation. Members of the Catholic Church and some Protestants devoted special efforts toward Jewish conversion until after World War II through the congregations of Notre Dame de Sion, the Paulists, and the Jesuits in Hungary and Vienna (Kuehnelt-Leddihn, 1946, p.220). The young intellectuals who were thus attracted to the majority faith were not, however, always the victims of proselytization. They were often confused, alienated, and vulnerable. Usually they were of the first or second generation of emancipated Jews who angrily rejected their own "medieval" faith and were unable to exist within the then-prevailing Jewish community life-style, or could not comfortably remain irreligious Jews. They yearned for a faith and commitment which conformed to their modern world. Moreover, to compound their confusion, they were often poorly informed about the traditional values of their own faith. Hence preaching, propagandizing, and teaching fell upon receptive ears and offered each individual a way to solve his own personal psychological or social dilemmas. The young men to be discussed in these pages came to conversion in this setting. Most were bright and discovered their passage to a new faith through intellectual as well as emotional paths, although not always.

David Drach

The conversion of David Drach in 1827 was one of the more scandalous within the Jewish community because of his family connections. He was a brilliant young author and teacher at the first public school for Jewish children, founded in 1819 in Paris. He was also the son-in-law of Emanuel (Menachim) Deutz, Chief Rabbi of France.

Drach was born in 1791 in Alsace and educated there until his father, who wanted him to become a rabbi, sent him away to various schools where he excelled in his studies. However, his associations and education were entirely in Yiddish or Hebrew and within the Jewish community. In early adolescence he came into direct contact with Catholic society and became curious about French culture. Because of his father's obdurate opposition to this curiosity, he was forced to study Greek and Latin clandestinely. Drach, in his account of this period, claimed that this curiosity was really his propensity and desire for Christianity and that that was why he disobeyed his father. His initial contact with Christians led him to study the Catholic religion and he engaged in lengthy discussions with a parish priest. He expressed an interest in conversion early, but as Drach wrote, "God had not planned my conversion so soon" (Drach, 1828).

The priests felt that the applicant was too young to take such a major step. He therefore returned to his Jewish studies and to his planned career. Two years later, despite his father's pleading that he remain in Alsace, Drach went to Paris and renewed his secular interests while working for a Catholic family. Drach said that "It was here [in Paris] that Providence arranged for me to be prepared for conversion." He became convinced that the Jews themselves had corrupted the Hebrew Scriptures (Old Testament). He finally converted to Catholicism, knowing the pain it would cause his family (especially his in-laws), because the "divine invitation to be a disciple required the sacrifice of mother, father, wife, brother and sisters" (Drach. 1825). Drach concluded his biographical account of his actions by saying that he wished not only to convince other Jews of their error but to "combat the irreligion which saturates our age" (Drach, 1825, pp.35-68).

Indeed, shortly after his conversion, Drach sought to persuade his wife to abandon her ancestral convictions. When that failed, he pretended to return to Judaism in order to gain his wife's trust and confidence and secure the custody of his children. When he was unable to obtain custody, he brought a bitter lawsuit against his wife, claiming his paternal rights to his children. He won in the courts, and his children were duly baptized and raised as Catholics (Klein, 1951, 83-87; c.f. Szjakowski, 1965, 55).

Drach became a prolific writer for the Church, directing bitter polemics against the Jews. He was friendly with Louis Veuillot, vitriolic anti-semite and ultramontane of mid-nineteenth century France (Isser, 1981). As with many converts, Drach needed to demonstrate his commitment by converting others, especially his fellow Jews (Drach, 1827, 1833). He was one of those converts who was possessed by intense self-hate, related to his struggles with his father in earlier years. The paternal decision directing the boy to the rabbinate and the arguments over secular learning that Drach related revealed inter-generational conflicts that could lead only to enormous guilt as a result of his non-conforming behavior. This led to his vicious attacks upon Judaism, which were essentially attacks upon his own origins and past (Isser & Schwartz, 1983).

Drach's invective was so filled with loathing that he was passionately disliked by the Jewish community. At his death, this obituary reflected the Jews' attitude toward him:

> As an apostate he [Drach] wished to ingratiate himself with those whose ranks he joined and to lull all suspicion of insincerity, bitterly attacked the deserted coreligionists and contributed his share towards fostering prejudice against Jews and Judaism (London *Jewish Chronicle*, 10 March 1865).

Simon Deutz

As a celebrated convert, Drach was widely accepted in Catholic legitimist circles, which impressed his brother-in-law, Simon Deutz, who also converted to Roman Catholicism. Accounts of the latter's conversion differ sharply. Deutz himself claimed that he was drawn to the majority faith because he hoped to hurt Drach, "who had ruined the happy life of his sister" (Szajkowski, 1965, p.55). Contradictory to this, but probably closer to the truth was Drach's assessment of Deutz's motives. Deutz, Drach claimed, had become secularized and alienated from his own traditions through prolonged study of eighteenth century philosophers. He abandoned his beliefs and became confused and troubled. Thus vulnerable, he was easily converted in 1828 when he was twenty-six years old (Drach, 1828, pp.11-15; Szajkowski, 1965). Unlike his brother-in-law, however, Simon did not indulge himself in self hate.

As the son of the Chief Rabbi, Simon's conversion was a particular source of satisfaction to the Church, and the Roman authorities duly utilized his services, sending him on delicate Papal missions. For his part, Deutz claimed that he tried, from his new position, to persuade the Pope to ease the conditions of Jews in the Papal States. Unfortunately, his efforts were to no avail. Frustrated and disappointed, he went to the United States, where his efforts to organize a Catholic publishing firm also failed. At the end of 1830, he returned to Europe, going to London and then Rome. He became implicated in the conspiracy of legitimists led by the Duchesse de Berry to seize the French throne. However, he "betrayed" that cause to the existing Orleanist government in France. The affair, minor though it was, led to a small anti-Jewish campaign which was embarrassing to his father and to the Jewish commmunity. [For a full account of the affair, c.f. Szajkowski, 1965, pp.33-67.] Deutz, unlike the other apostates, ultimately returned to his original faith, subsequently married a Jewish woman, and, after a short sojourn in the United States and England, once more settled in France (Klein, 1951).

Jacob Libermann

Another example of the second generation Jew caught between the traditional encapsulated ghetto and the modern age of emancipation was Jacob Libermann. Unlike some of the other converts, Libermann became a significant figure in Catholic religious history. Like several of the other converts cited here, though, he was born in Alsace, the fifth son of Samson Libermann and Leah Haller. His mother died when he was only eleven years old. Although his father remarried and more children followed, Jacob seemed to have endured maternal deprivation. This felt lack in his life was expressed in his later life in his religious attachment to Mary and his sympathy for mothers. Jacob was his father's favorite child. Like David Drach, Jacob was directed by his father to study in the traditional Jewish Yeshiva to prepare for a career in the rabbinate. Also like Drach, Jacob attended secular schools while he was studying in Saverne, despite parental disapproval. He mastered Greek, Latin, and improved his French, and was able to read both modern and Enlightenment philosophers.

Jacob, like his older brothers before him, rebelled against his father's faith and ghetto life. He became a free thinker, a deist, and refrained from all religious observances. All this behavior, however, was deliberately concealed from his father. Meanwhile, his older brothers had converted to Catholicism in Paris, and the father, in despair, sent Jacob to dissuade them. While there, the young Jew met David Drach (through the Chief Rabbi, Deutz). Moved both by his brothers' example and the persuasive, though indiscreet proselytization of Drach, Jacob was baptized at the age of twenty-four years. As with other converts, he changed his name, from Jacob to Francois Marie Paul. In 1827, he entered the Sulpician seminary at Issy, but his epileptic attacks prevented his acceptance into the priesthood. He remained, however, at Issy teaching the novices. A meeting with Creole seminarians led to his interest in the former slaves from the West Indies. He founded a new society, the

Congregation of the Holy Spirit, which not only won Papal approval, but finally brought his ordination as a priest.

In 1848, Libermann's society merged with the Holy Ghost Fathers and became the missionaries of the Sacred Heart of Mary. Libermann became the Superior General of the new order. He inculcated the Congregation with what have become modern missionary principles: a fusion of spiritual teaching coupled with practical and economic service. He also avoided contact with the Jewish community by refraining from proselytization within it (Blanchard, I, 1960). Unlike Drach and others, Libermann seemed less guilt-ridden, although he was pained about his father's anguish over the conversion of his sons. Libermann died in 1852.

The Ratisbonnes

Two famous cases reflecting the conflicts of the second generation of Jews after Emancipation were those of Theodore and Alphonse Ratisbonne. Their conversions are of special interest because they recorded their experiences in great detail. Related after the fact, their autobiographies provided more insight than was available for the previous cases. In addition, they came from families that had assimilated into the mainstream of French culture, and who were no longer religiously observant. However, the prominent and wealthy Ratisbonnes **had** assumed leadership within the Jewish community of Alsace.

Theodore Ratisbonne, the elder of the brothers, was a young man rebelling against his foreordained role, seeking beliefs and a "cause" without quite knowing for what he was searching. Trying first one path and then another, he belatedly studied Jewish precepts, then philosophy. Led by a dynamic teacher, Theodore was proselytized slowly at first and then with increasing intensity as his involvement with his teacher and other non-Jews developed. His was an intellectual conversion, based on study and thought, and was concluded as a result of a low-key or "soft-sell" approach by those desiring to convert him.

Theodore's brother, Alphonse, some 12 years younger, was initially repelled by Theodore's conversion and broke relations with the apostate. However, he, too, converted to Catholicism as a young man. By contrast, however, Alphonse was subjected to an intensive campaign of proselytization, virtually a "siege," to which he succumbed in less than a week. While he protested to the last that he was "born a Jew and would die a Jew," he experienced a "miraculous" vision that resulted in his instantaneous conversion emotionally and prompt baptism religiously.

In the cases of both Ratisbonnes, their accounts were written after their respective conversions. As a result, some caution must be exercised in accepting all of the information, particularly of pre-conversion feelings, as completely true. Modern psychologists recognize that people who accept new views and/or adopt new behavior patterns have a need to reconcile pre-change ideas or behaviors with those held after such change. The reconciliation is needed to reduce tensions arising from cognitive dissonance.

Theodore Ratisbonne

Theodore was the second son of Adelaide (Cerfberr) and Auguste Ratisbonne, a family prominent in the banking and Jewish communities of Alsace in the early nineteenth century. In spite of the secular life-style of the family, Theodore was sent to a fashionable Jewish boarding school in Frankfurt in his early teens. He was taught to read Hebrew there, but nothing about God or religion. He reported later that at the time he felt a need for prayer, but mistakenly thought it was an adolescent's need to love. By his later teens, Theodore felt that religious observances were a joke, that there was little dignity in the synagogue, and felt ashamed of being called a Jew. He thereupon decided to withdraw from the Jewish community, a matter in which his father gave him complete freedom (T.Ratisbonne, I, 1904, p.25).

If Theodore had little affinity for his religion, what **were** his resources? He was a daydreamer and not an ambitious student either at boarding school, which he hated, or in his banking studies with the Foulds, a prominent Parisian Jewish banking family. The Foulds, with whom he lived as part of the family, also failed to profess any religious tendencies. Theodore at 16 was free, unsupervised, without goals, without religion, with limitless credit, and bored by his work at the bank.

In December 1818, his mother, dearly loved and his "surest protection" even at a distance, died. The intensity of Theodore's grief was such that he was unable to recover from the shock. He had lost what he held most dear, and suddenly became aware of the fragility of life. For the first time, he envisioned the philosophical problem of death and uncertainty of what followed. Solitary as a child, the youth was inconsolable and lost after his mother's death. In his memoirs, Theodore wrote:

> How much a religious word was needed at that point! I suffered from an indefinable malady. But I didn't know one man, one book that could teach me about divine things. I reacted with aversion to whoever spoke to me of Christianity, for I had prejudged that as idolatry. As for Judaism, I was disabused of it, and the synagogue seemed to me to pose a barrier between God and myself (I, p.28).

He was seized with the notion that the only way to remain in touch with his mother's soul was to study religion. A young rabbi came one or twice a week to teach him to pray in Hebrew and to explain the holidays and ceremonies, but Theodore remain uninspired. He once asked the rabbi about the promise of a Messiah and whether the Christians had any reason to support their belief that he had already come. The rabbi responded, "If you want to believe it, I can't stop you." With that attitude, it is hardly surprising that the lessons left little impression on the young man and did little to reduce his grief.

In addition to melancholy, Theodore continued to lack motivation or initiative, all common symptoms of depression. Sent home by M. Fould after more than two years of listlessness, Theodore, realizing that he had to do something, sought and received permission to study for the baccalaureat en route to becoming a lawyer. At age 20, tormented in his soul and still drifting, he began to seek answers to the questions he had about life's purposes. Becoming ever more austere and solitary in his behavior, he searched for answers and truths in the Masons, in science, and in philosophy, becoming more and more disenchanted as he continued. In his memoirs, Theodore wrote that he spent a great deal of time in solitary walks during this period.

After one such walk, the thought came to Theodore that a powerful intelligence had had to create the heavens and to preside over their harmonious progress. At that moment of anguish and apparent insight, he called out to the God of his childhood, he later recalled, "O mysterious Being, Creator, Sire, Lord, if you exist, have pity on your creature. Show me the road which leads to truth, and I will pledge to consecrate my life to you!" (T.Ratisbonne, I, 1904, p.32)

Meanwhile, with all his perplexed preoccupations, Theodore was not making progress toward his degree. He left Strasbourg toward the end of 1822 for Paris where, despite his torments, he enjoyed himself at the theatre and in other pleasures. An "interior voice" finally told him to leave Paris and return to Strasbourg. On his return, he enrolled in the local University. A fellow student suggested that he take a course in philosophy with M. Bautain, a zealous Catholic and dynamic teacher. This Theodore did in 1823, learning Bautain's view of ideal Christianity without realizing it. After graduating at last later that year, he traveled, and then resumed his studies with Bautain the following year.

Theodore believed at that point that Bautain had shown himself and other Jewish students the way to be reconciled with Judaism. He began to observe the Sabbath with great rigidity, and weekly, "despite the sarcasm of his family," went to the synagogue on Friday evenings. However, an "invincible malaise" was entrenched in his heart, and Theodore continued to be tormented. He experienced boredom in prayer and "an insurmountable disgust" with his religion. He concluded that Jews were a "family of pariahs in the middle of Christian nations," but maintained that he still regarded his people with affection. In response, M. Bautain wrote him that "Christian dogmas are the development, the application, the accomplishment of the announced truths of Judaism" (T.Ratisbonne, I, 1904, pp.60-61).

The correspondence between the young man and his teacher continued for some time, with Theodore unable to accept the concept of the Trinity and Bautain insistent that Christianity represented the perfection of Mosaic Judaism. The latter developed a rationale to demonstrate to Theodore that belief in the Trinity was simply an extension of ancient Judaism. By the end of 1824, Theodore was convinced of the veracity of Bautain's argument and crossed the line of intellectual conversion. Soon after he received his bachelor of laws degree in January 1825, he entered a Catholic church for the first time.

Meanwhile, Theodore's father had obtained a post for him as director of the Jewish community school in Strasbourg. Reluctant at first to accept because of his antipathy to Judaism, Theodore finally accepted it at the urging of Bautain because he could then lead the younger generation to the "true" road, i.e., to convert them. Writing of this episode, Theodore said that "The perspective of this good, with my burning desire to transmit the light I have received, made me determined to accept this work of beneficence, and from then on, I devoted myself to it entirely" (T.Ratisbonne, I, pp.67-68).

While directing the school, Theodore was also working on his law thesis and was being pressed to marry a fine and wealthy young woman from Vienna. He was irresolute and confused about the marriage, in a dilemma for some months. There is no further mention of the proposed marriage in the memoirs. He received his law license in early 1826 and then decided to study medicine, which he did for two years. At the same time, he was becoming more infatuated with Catholicism.

Although Theodore had intellectually accepted much of Catholic philosophy, it was not until 1825, when he was ill, that he was able even to pronounce the names of Jesus and Mary. At that point, he later claimed, "The ineradicable tenderness of my mother made me find divine the same kind of love of Mary" (T.Ratisbonne, I, 1904, p.69). He also found a "true mother" in Mlle. Humann, a close friend of Bautain, and equally committed to bringing Theodore into the Church as a practicing Christian. He loved her intensely, writing that "she made me understand the Holy Virgin; and the more I loved her, the more I was drawn to Jesus Christ, the focus of true love" (T.Ratisbonne, I, 1904, p.76). At Mlle. Humann's suggestion, Theodore kept a daily diary in which he wrote his innermost thoughts. This eased his gradual transition into his new life as a Christian. Theodore was secretly baptized on 14 April 1827, but continued to speak publicly to his fellow Jews, inserting Christian concepts in a subtle manner in his addresses. He viewed his formal entrance into the Church as comparable to the movement of the Israelites from slavery in Egypt to the promised land, and saw no impropriety in sharing his new "knowledge" in a veiled way.

Theodore received his first communion secretly in September 1827 at Mayence, taking the names Marie-Louis-Joseph-Theodore. M. Bautain and Mlle. Humann served as godparents. At his confirmation some weeks later, he added the names Simon and Peter (T.Ratisbonne, I, 1904, p.86). He later noted that the idea of entering the priesthood first emerged after his return from Mayence.

Theodore finally revealed his conversion to an assemblage of Jewish students and their parents. His co-religionists reviled him, and his father was deeply pained and humiliated by his son's surreptitious actions. Theodore could or would not perceive that his successes in Jewish education were obtained under false pretenses and were, therefore, objectionable to the community. In his closing remarks on this controversial occasion, Theodore said: "You approve the works, but deny the faith that produced them. You recognize the tree by its fruits, but the tree that bears bad fruit is not good and the tree that bears good fruit cannot be bad" (T.Ratisbonne, I, 1904, p.94).

By 1828, Theodore had embarked on studies leading to his ordination as a priest in December 1830. Following the death of his beloved Mlle. Humann in 1836, he dedicated himself to the service of Mary, "the heavenly Mother of Jesus" (T.Ratisbonne, I, 1904, p.167). In 1841, he formed the community of "The Ladies of Good Works," and also the "Priests of St. Louis." The following year, he was received by Pope Gregory XVI, who gave him honors for his book, *History of St. Bernard*, and also granted Theodore's request for a mission to work toward the conversion of Jews. His missionary activity began in earnest after the conversion of his brother Alphonse in 1842.

Within a few years he had 80 women in his community, all of whom took a vow of service to Jesus "and his divine Mother, Our Lady of Zion." They further promised to "show all possible zeal to the conversion of the Jewish people" (T.Ratisbonne, I, 1904, pp.352-353). The community became the Institute of Notre Dame de Sion (Our Lady of Zion) in 1847, the name again reflecting Theodore's insensitivity to his former co-religionists. The primary work of the Institute was to incorporate Catholic principles in education, accompanied by active proselytizing. The order's formal status was granted in 1874.

Pius IX gave Theodore the title of Apostolic Missionary in 1851. He continued to write profusely, was recognized as a charismatic speaker, and was constantly refining his views and practices as an educator. On the negative side, Theodore was involved in both the Mallet-Bluth scandal (*supra*) and the Elisabeth Linneweil affair (*supra*). He remained active, despite his problems of financing and excessive religiosity, until his death in 1884.

Alphonse Ratisbonne

Alphonse, younger brother of Theodore, was the ninth of the ten Ratisbonne children. He was only four when their mother died, and, while he had affectionate care from his father, uncle, and older sisters, was deprived of the closer nurturing his older siblings had had. Unlike Theodore, he left few recollections of his earliest feelings and childhood years. Also unlike Theodore, he attended a fashionable Protestant school as a youth, the Royal College of Strasbourg, and received even less religious training in Judaism. Alphonse **did** note in his memoirs that he was very upset, at age eleven, when Theodore converted to Catholicism.

By July 1830, when Alphonse was sixteen, his father died. His uncle became the patriarch of the family, the second father who assumed leadership and direction of the children. Certain poignant factors emerge from this history of Alphonse's childhood and youth. He was raised without the strong direction and love the older children had enjoyed. His mother's death meant substantial deprivation at a most critical point in his early development. Because his older sisters attempted to serve as her substitutes, however, he remained closely attached to those close in age to him throughout his life. An additional traumatic factor in Alphonse's youth was Theodore's conversion, a dreadful emotional blow for the entire family that sapped energy and probably attention from the younger children. Finally, when he was sixteen, again a crucial time in his development, the boy's father died, removed precipitously when most needed as a model.

His uncle Louis, expecting Alphonse to accept the duties of his family as well as its religious and communal obligations, accordingly determined that the youth should enter the banking business at Strasbourg. He was first sent to Paris, where he studied law, and by 1834 received his degree and was licensed. He then returned to Strasbourg and became a partner in the bank. Like Theodore, and in spite of the generosity and affection of his uncle, Alphonse detested banking. However, just as he had accepted the position in the bank, he also assumed the expected community obligations. He joined committees to provide charity and "regeneration" for poor Jews, and was active in raising money to ameliorate existing poverty. Zealous in his charitable efforts, Alphonse was equally firm in rejecting his religion as a belief.

Alphonse's behavior until the age of twenty-seven certainly appeared normal and even happy. While he did not perform brilliantly at school, he succeeded sufficiently well to avoid anger or upset in his family. As for his career, he accepted the training and business for which he was predestined, despite a lack of enthusiasm, and did not exhibit any overt rebellion. Instead, Alphonse sought the approbation of his peer group. He was outer-directed, and loved pleasure, parties, and other entertainments. Alphonse also found a measure of security, warmth, and protection within the bosom of his family. However, the imperative to transcend his family ties and strike out to achieve independence was never attempted. That would have meant loosening or cutting his emotional and psychological bonds, something that Alphonse could not do, even to attain a fuller sense of identity or his optimum level of development.

When he was twenty-seven, the family pressured Alphonse to marry in an alliance that would cement family and economic ties. A betrothal was arranged between him and his niece, Flore, the daughter of Adolph, his eldest brother. As Flore was only 16, it was decided to postpone the wedding for a time. While the family rejoiced at the prospective alliance, and Alphonse was ostensibly delighted, he was suddenly seized with feelings of depression and the added symptoms of chest pains, general malaise, and deep melancholia — no doubt all expressions of his deep inner conflicts.

After much uncertainty and even reluctance to leave his "beloved" family, his friends, and his charitable activities, Alphonse was persuaded to take a Mediterranean trip in the hope of improving his health. His first stop was Naples where, he reported in his letters home, he felt very bleak. Melancholia and loneliness gripped him even more strongly on New Year's Eve of 1841-42 in the midst of all the night's gaiety and revelry. Soon after, still despairing, Alphonse made an unanticipated side trip to Rome. In the course of sightseeing there, he visited both the Church of Aracoeli on the Capitoline Hill and the Jewish ghetto of Rome. He had an intense emotional reaction at the Church, which his guide claimed was a common experience. At the ghetto, on the other hand, he was appalled at the misery in which his co-religionists lived.

While touring the various churches, galleries, and catacombs, he encountered a childhood friend, Gustave de Bussières (who himself had recently converted from his Lutheran faith to a more fundamentalist Pietist creed). De Bussières promptly tried to convert Alphonse to the Protestant sect of which he was now a member.

Gustave then introduced Alphonse to his brother, Theodore de Bussières) married, as it happened to the niece of the Mlle. Humann who had been so influential in Theodore Ratisbonne's conversion), who was a recent convert to Catholicism. The latter was determined to persuade Alphonse of the veracity and grandeur of **his** faith.

At this point, 16 January 1842, Theodore de Bussières asked Alphonse to wear a holy medal that had a portrait of Mary on one side and a cross on the other. He also asked the younger man to recite a prayer, the *Memorare*. Alphonse mockingly accepted the gift and reluctantly acceded to the requests. In correspondence a few months later, Alphonse mentioned his regret that he had no Hebrew prayer that he could ask be recited in return.

Alphonse, already emotionally troubled, lonely, and somewhat flattered by the attention of the de Bussières brothers — in a word, vulnerable — was gradually and not too subtly being influenced by the Catholic faith. He wore the medal with the a mother image, the Virgin, and repeated the words of the prayer continually and mechanically. Acceding to a further request by de Bussières, he copied the words of the prayer on paper, a motor act that further reinforced the prayer in his mind. De Bussières, determined to convert his young acquaintance, requested his own children and friends to pray for such a conversion. Among those friends was the Comte de la Ferronays, who died very shortly thereafter.

On the night of 19 January, Alphonse recorded, he was startled awake by the image of a large black cross that was similar, it turned out, to the one on the reverse of the holy medal he had been given. It was apparent that autosuggestion had been effective and that the image had become a reality to him. The next day, he accompanied Theodore de Bussières on an errand at the Church of San Andrea della Fratte, about five blocks from the Spanish Steps. De Bussières was making funeral arrangements for his suddenly departed dear friend, the Comte. Casually

entering the church, Alphonse wandered into one of the
deserted chapels that line the walls of the church. He there
had a sudden vision of Mary and was instantly "converted."
Witnesses to the event described Alphonse as appearing to
be in a state of ecstasy, shedding tears of happiness while he
described his exaltation. He demanded that he be taken to a
priest immediately, seized his medal, kissing it and
repeatedly crying, "I have seen her!"

Alphonse was certain that the Comte de la Ferronays had
prayed for him and interceded for him. He thought of his
elder brother, the convert Theodore, with a newly found joy.
Even in his excitement, however, he knew that the rest of his
family and his friends would turn against him, and perhaps
even ridicule him. The same evening, following his
miraculous vision, Alphonse requested instruction in the
Catholic faith. He was subsequently baptized on 31 January
and, like Theodore, took the name Marie.

The news of the miracle spread quickly. The Church,
however, did not accept the miracle without a grave and
penetrating inquiry. Directed by the Cardinal Vicar himself,
the Church's investigating committee concluded that the
miracle was authentic. Alphonse did not wait for the
conclusion of the hearing; he went to Paris to visit his brother
Theodore, and then entered a novitiate at Toulouse.

Conversion provided Alphonse with the means of
avoiding his obligations and of achieving independence, but
at the terrible cost of denying his past, wounding his family,
and abandoning his fiancée. (He did offer to go through
with the marriage if she converted, but, of course, the offer
was spurned by the family.) He sought admission to the

Society of Jesus in 1842 as a novice, and was ordained a priest in 1848. In 1852, he left the Jesuits to join his brother, Abbé Theodore, in the latter's missionary efforts to convert Jews, Protestants, and secular Catholics. This work led to the founding of the religious Order of Our Lady of Zion and the Fathers of St. Pierre of Zion, in which Alphonse played an active role. Leaving Paris ultimately, he continued to serve the church in Jerusalem, where he founded Ecce Homo, a chapter of the Order. Alphonse died among his beloved nuns and priests in Jerusalem in 1884, within months of his brother Theodore's death.

Other cases

Cases such as Alphonse's, of miraculous religious visions, were not rare. However, in more secular and scientifically-oriented societies, such incidents were greeted with greater skepticism. The apparition that Bernadette reported at Lourdes in 1858, for example, provoked enormous controversy initially among the French before it was ultimately accepted as genuine.

Another instance was the strange coincidence of Madelaine Semer, a religious mystic. She had been converted to a devout belief in Catholicism from a former commitment to rational agnosticism. One of her visions occurred while she worked for a then older Flore (the former fiancée of Alphonse), who had married a wealthy Jew. Madelaine was devoted to Flore until her death in 1912. In Semer's case, her visions were regarded as genuine but not miraculous. They were seen as "the true mark of God's love" (Isser & Schwartz, 1983).

More recent cases of visions recounted in the twentieth century were also considered as individual mystical experiences rather than as miracles. One such case was Max Jacob, poet and surrealist painter, who was proselytized by a priest. Following several talks, Jacob told how, upon returning home from such a talk one evening, he saw the figure of Jesus hanging on the cross on the wall of his apartment. Rushing out to see the priest the next morning, he peremptorily begged for baptism, probably with the same rapturous excitement as Alphonse Ratisbonne had exhibited earlier. However, as was to be expected in 1934, his request was denied. A year later, Jacob again reported seeing the vision and once more demanded baptism. This second time, his request was honored. He devoted himself, after his conversion, to art education. Ironically, he died because of his Jewish origins in a concentration camp (Kuehnelt-Leddihn, 1946, p.213).

One of the more notorious conversions was that of Eugenio Zolli, Chief Rabbi of Rome. On the Day of Atonement (Yom Kippur) in 1944, Zolli had a vision which he described for us:

In the evening there was the last service, and I was there with two assistants, one on my right and the other on my left. But I felt so far withdrawn from the ritual that I let others recite the prayers and sing. I was conscious of neither joy nor sorrow; I was devoid of thought and feeling. My heart lay as though dead in my breast. And just then I saw with my mind's eye a meadow sweeping upward, with bright grass but with no flowers. In this meadow I saw Jesus Christ clad in a white mantle, and beyond His head the blue sky. I experienced the greatest interior peace... . It was a few days after this that I resigned my post in the Israelite community and went to a quite unknown priest to receive instruction. An interval of some weeks elapsed, until the 13th of February, when I received the Sacrament of Baptism and was incorporated into the Catholic Church, the Mystical Body of Jesus Christ (Zolli, 1954).

However, there is another view of Zolli's conversion that suggests that perhaps his change was precipitated by motives other than religious idealism or visions. Zolli had been accused of cowardice by his congregation because, during World War II, he sought asylum in the Vatican. After the war, he responded in vindictive anger to criticism by his fellow Jews and showed his gratitude to the Church by converting (Newman, 1945).

Regardless of his true motives, Zolli's explanations for his conversion echo the sentiments expressed earlier by Drach, Libermann, and indeed he seemed to have employed almost the same language and imagery common to all Catholic converts: of being born again, of God's intervention, mystical union in God's love, and new strengths developed in the spiritual bonds of Christ (Zolli, 1954; c.f. Raissa Maritain, 1946). These ideas were sincerely felt, but they are a reflection not of the neophyte's motives and true feelings before conversion, but the expression of his true alternation of character. The similarities of language and ideas reveal how deep and genuine the conversion was. Each man had completely absorbed the rhetoric and logic of the new faith.

An even more interesting aspect of the alternation of character can be seen in the arguments of these converts to their fellow Jews. The letters of Drach, Libermann (Blanchard, 1960; Drach, 1828, 1829, 1833), and the pamphlets of Theodore Ratisbonne (Ratisbonne, 1868, 1878), carried the identical arguments and analysis of the Bible and Hebrew language that were standard Catholic belief, but which had long been rejected by the Jewish community as both wrong and antisemitic. Indeed, some of their arguments revealed fundamental errors about Judaism, which as former Jews they should not have made. Their language and statements were often offensive, and their translations of Hebrew faulty. The same statements that had been bitterly assailed by Alphonse and Theodore **before** conversion, suddenly became the language of their ardent attempts to convert their former co-religionists. This alternation displayed how deeply emotional their so-called intellectual conversions really were. The same phenomenon was noted by the sociologist, James Beckford (1976) in his study of the Jehovah's Witnesses. He found that converts, in the course of adopting their new faith, assumed also the common language, imagery, and attitudes consonant with it.

Unlike the Ratisbonnes, who as Jews had been wholly immersed in the secular world, Drach, Deutz, and Libermann gained materially from conversion. They were sons of prominent but poor Jewish families living within an isolated community. Their professions as teachers or rabbis were moderately paid. Fellow Jews noted these facts with great asperity so that Drach himself felt constrained to refute their charges of profiteering (Drach, 1838). The sincerity of these conversions should not be doubted, but the social and economic mobility, and the freedom to move into the modern world, gained by conversion, should not be ignored.

The case of the Ratisbonnes was different. They gained nothing materially from their conversions. For them, the benefits were psychological. Conversion resolved deep-seated conflicts, and feelings of hostility and guilt.

Discussion

Although we want to focus on the Ratisbonne brothers' conversions in this discussion, there is one element involved in several of the cases presented that should be noted. That element is deception. Drach pretended to return to Judaism; Libermann deceived his father; and Theodore Ratisbonne deceived his father and community while head of the Jewish school. There is also some question of how genuine a motive Deutz had in his conversion. We do not assert that deception is common in all conversions, but its presence in these emotionally-based instances, encouraged in some cases by the proselytizers, is related to the deception seen in many of the conversions to modern-day cults, which will be discussed in the next chapter.

The conversions of the Ratisbonne brothers were direct results of proselytization — one gradual and the other intensive in nature. Theodore's conversion was an intellectual one, based on study and thought, but its roots lay in his desire to escape his fate and to ascertain his own identity. Alphonse's conversion, by contrast, was allegedly miraculous as well as instantaneous. It, too, provided an avenue of escape from his obligations and an opportunity to achieve independence. Mortimer Ostow, a psycho-analytically-oriented psychiatrist, offered to us the hypothesis that the brothers may have been latent homo-sexuals, possibly even with a mutual attraction. Ostow noted that a precipitating factor en route to conversion for both men was an impending marriage, and also that they each took the unusual step — for a male — of adopting the name Marie (Private communication, 1981). [We might add that Libermann also adopted the name Marie, although as one of his middle names.]

For Theodore, his new status as a committed convert brought him praise, warmth, and even adulation from new friends and persons important in the French community. His new identity became so complete that gradually he became a different personality from the alienated, introverted young Jew he had been. All ties with his past, including those with his family, were severed. Weber (1956), Tucker (1968), and others have attempted to explicate the qualities of the charismatic leader, such as Theodore became (as can be seen in his career after 1830). (Libermann, also a physically frail young man, similarly found a useful and later even important role provided for him within the Church after his conversion.) Theodore's belief in the righteousness of his mission, typical of charismatic leaders, rationalized for him all his excesses of zeal and provided inspiration to those who followed his teachings. The high level of activity that he exhibited, along with his charisma, is typical of the hypomanic personality (Ostow, 1982).

Characteristics of the hypomanic personality, according to Ostow, include: a lack of "the capacity for intimacy so that despite ... attractiveness, generosity, and popularity, [the individual] is seldom a good parent or spouse;" an ability to "see potentialities beyond those that are visible to the non-hypomanic; yet ... sufficiently realistic to warrant being taken seriously;" and contributions to society by virtue of industriousness and creativity. "In addition, because he possesses so many attributes of leadership, he is often accepted as a leader" (Ostow, 1982, pp.224-226). Theodore's hold on his converts — Catholic, non-Christian, and non-believer alike — was enormous, and many proved their unquestioning obedience and love by taking religious vows and joining his order. His constant writing was a reflection of his two internal needs: one to maintain his pastoral leadership and authority; the other to rationalize his own role and relationship to God and the Church. Hence, he maintained a constant stream of letters, instructions, and essays, in addition to the continual travel and supervision of the well-established religious houses he had founded, to the end of his days.

With Alphonse, there was a somewhat different picture. Psychologists and psychiatrists have looked at his "miraculous conversion" from a non-theological viewpoint. William James (1957/1902) raised the question of subliminal influences at work in his comments on the event. Morton Prince (1906) challenged James' position and raised the possibility that Alphonse had been in a trance-like state related to a condition of mental disintegration. Alphonse's own lengthy description of his experience corresponds to Prince's analysis of the trance state, to Scobie's perceptions of suggestibility and hysteria (1975), and to Ostow's statement that almost every participant in a mystical trance "describes himself as approaching, seeing, being awed by, touching or being touched by, or being united with, a divinity. ... That the experience is essentially indescribably, 'ineffable' is the term generally used" (1975, p.2533). This "ineffable" state is likened to a dissociated one resembling those seen in an hysterical attack at the onset of schizophrenia.

Another line of thought raises other questions about Alphonse's conversion. Why did he accept the medal given him by de Bussiéres and copy the prayer at his new friend's behest? Was this another example of his desire for peer approval? Was de Bussiéres' unremitting pressure so effective that Alphonse, in a state of personal futility, simply surrendered his will to resist? Was the fact that Alphonse had a vision of Mary related to the early loss of his mother? In the recitation of his conversion, he twice referred to himself as a "newborn infant" — what we would call today "born again" — which suggests that Mary was perceived as such a replacement. Was there a link between Alphonse's sudden conversion and an unconscious but long-standing resentment of his father (and perhaps his uncle as a surrogate father) who had directed his future? (Carmelle, I, 1977, pp.14-15) The negative feeling has been widely reported as a motive for conversion, even though it may be unconscious (Miller, 1971; Salzman, 1953).

Lonely, seeking autonomy, and faced with difficult decisions, Goguel (in Guitton, 1964) suggested that Alphonse could not find harmony within himself, but only through an external source. Both Goguel, as quoted by Guitton, and Guitton (1964) hypothesized that Alphonse had a love-hate ambivalence regarding his personal life and his Jewishness that predisposed him to conversion. Ostow and others averred that the ambivalence was handled by turning away from the source of distress, by "retreating into a state of narcissism in which the external world ceases to exist, recreating a more ideal relation — now with the superparent, God — and conveniently transferring the stamp of reality from actual reality to fantasy" (Guitton, 1964, p.80).

In his recollections, Alphonse described himself as a dutiful son and nephew. He admitted to a negative view of the leaders of the Jewish community, who he perceived as hypocrites, and of Judaism — indeed all religion. There are no comments on acts of rebellion or even fantasies of rebellion in his memoirs. There are no expressions of hatred of his father that might have stimulated him to convert as an act of defiance. He appears to have been what Marcia (1966) called a "foreclosure subject." Therefore, we must accept Alphonse's view that he experienced a genuine miraculous conversion or deduce as others have done that the vision was a product of the interaction of proselytization of a suggestible individual and his emotional instability, and was the mechanism by which Alphonse could resolve his approach-avoidance conflicts most expediently.

Morton Prince (1906) considered the recital of conversion experiences and their antecedents to be unreliable because of the intense emotional excitement involved and the fact that such narratives were invariably written from a religious, rather than an objective and psychological, point of view. Much of our knowledge of the proselytization activities that led to the conversion of both Theodore and Alphonse, and to the conversion of others mentioned here, comes from such post facto writings. Certainly Alphonse's writings clearly stress mystical and religious aspects, even to the point of emphasizing the quarter-hour that separated his insistence that he was "born a Jew and would die a Jew" and the instant of his conversion (Guitton, 1964, p.115). Nevertheless, the attention paid by psychiatrists and psychologists to both events, combined with the subjects' own views, provide valuable insights to the differing techniques of proselytization and their varying effects on individuals. These insights are extremely helpful as we examine modern conversions in the next chapter.

CHAPTER IV — CONVERSION AND CONTEMPORARY
CULTS

The majority of case histories we have analyzed in the past chapters were Jews and the incidents occurred mostly in nineteenth century France. These conversions involved established religious institutions, and existed in an earlier time frame and in a distinctly different physical and social environment. Nevertheless, psychologically, we could draw some analogies and even extrapolate some insights applicable to contemporary problems of the United States.

The present growth of cults and the attraction of young people to them, the revival of interest in fundamental Christianity, Eastern religions, and esoteric "psychological" groups such as *est* and Life-Spring, compel us to confront the whole issue of proselytization and conversion once more, but in a different light. Although the plethora of cults have been a part of American socio-religious tradition, few have made the transition to "respectable" religion or "quaint sect."

Fractional religious development was fostered by frontier life and the pluralistic society of the nineteenth century, and the relative absence of rigid structure in religion, even within the Roman Catholic Church, as compared with European society. The Shakers, Old Order Amish, House of David, Oneida Community, and Hutterites were all tolerated to some degree as reflecting religious diversity appropriate to our diverse population. There was resistance to the Mormons (Church of Latter-Day Saints), Christian Science, Jehovah's Witnesses, and the Father Divine Movement, because of their intensive proselytizing efforts, but today, they, too, are tolerated and accepted as variants of mainstream religion (Kanter, 1972; Kephart, 1982).

How many of our contemporary cults can achieve even such limited acceptance is debatable. Even relatively innocuous groups today are sometimes regarded with suspicion because of questionable practices and scandals associated with the tragedy of Jonestown or the indictments directed toward the Church of Scientology. Further, the recruitment practices of some sects smack either of enticement or irregularity which have engendered deprogramming by angry families. Thus, even cults which previously would have been ignored or perhaps tolerated are now greeted with animosity. Of even greater significance is the fact that the most concerted recruiting efforts of contemporary religious movements have been directed toward middle class young adults and college students; and in the communal organization of these groups, the family relationships are severed.

However, an assessment and comparison of conversion and proselytization on the part of modern religious practices requires an examination of the cults themselves.

The Cults

Describing the modern cults when there are 1000 to 3000 of them is not an easy matter as they vary in size, life-style, orientation (socio-political, spiritual, self-improvement), and activities. They also differ in recruiting techniques, although most have very persuasive advocates. The one thing they tend to have in common is the conviction of each group that it has the sole "correct" route to salvation or self-actualization.

> The legitimacy of cult leaders' contentions that they possess a superior knowledge and virtue is seriously weakened by the insistence of each that he alone has the revealed word of God, of perfect knowledge and understanding of the cosmos and man's place in it. ... Inasmuch as cult leaders and their representatives to the public are not questioned about this, their intolerance of each other's religious beliefs and of society's religions is ignored by those writing in their defense (E.Levine, 1985, p.117).

It would be impossible to provide a detailed view of even the dozen or so best-known groups in a few pages, so that what follows is essentially a series of objective thumbnail sketches to familiarize the reader with characteristics of the major groups.

The "Unification Church"

The Holy Spirit Association for the Unification of World Christianity (the Unification Church) was founded by the Rev. Sun Myung Moon in 1954. Its theology is contained in the *Divine Principle* (a description of a new messiah whose goal will be to unify the world's cultures and religions into one family with Christianity as its base), and was written by

Moon himself (McGowan, 1979). Devotees of the Unification Church are popularly known as "Moonies." Active around the world, the Unification Church is a highly structured organization that is often cited as the prototype of cults. The life-style is principally a communal one, and the major activities of most members are fund-raising and recruiting. The Unification Church also publishes three newspapers (*News World* in New York, a Spanish language daily, and the *Washington Times* in Washington, D.C.), has a UHF-TV station in New York, owns large real estate parcels, and operates a number of successful fishing enterprises.

Mose Durst, head of the Unification Church in the United States, said, in a December 1980 television interview (WTAF-TV, Ch.29, Philadelphia), that the goals of the Church are "to build universal love ... [and] express it through social action" and to encourage interracial marriage en route to creating the one world-wide family. He emphasized teaching, education, inspiration, service, and worship as Church activities. Despite Durst's assertion in late 1980 that fund-raising activities such as flower- and candy-selling would be phased out, members were still to be found selling on street corners and from door-to-door in business establishments (Herbut, 1980). He also denied that the Church used deceptive recruiting practices, "brain-washing" techniques, or that it separates members from their families.

The Church of Scientology

The largest of the cult groups is the Church of Scientology, a "psychotherapy" cult founded and headed by L.Ron Hubbard (until his death early in 1986). An outgrowth of the Dianetics movement, also begun by

Hubbard, the Church of Scientology alleges that its courses can help the individual to improve his/her life by attaining the goal of self-understanding (Hopkins, 1969). The courses vary in price, but completing each course brings one nearer to the goal and to high status in Scientology's hierarchy.

The novice or "preclear" takes introductory courses at a local Scientology church, the object of which is to create social bonds; allow the neophyte to express feelings spontaneously; and invest heavily of time, money, and emotions (Stark & Bainbridge, 1980). The ideology focuses on theories of metaphysics and reincarnation, and is concerned with the "thetan" or spirit rather than the mind. According to Wallis (1975),

> In the course of its many reincarnations the thetan had experienced many traumatic events which progressively weighed it down, causing it to lose its spiritual abilities and awareness and leaving the individual believing he was merely a body. Scientology practices claimed to liberate or "rehabilitate" the thetan, clearing away "mental mass" which limited its activity, until the individual became again an Operating Thetan, able to travel independently of the body, and with other supernatural abilities (pp.95-96).

One either conforms to Scientology dogma or is expelled. Those outside the organization who criticize it are often harassed despite attempts in the past to portray Scientology as a religious and humanitarian group. There is, however, no deity that is worshipped, nor is there any ritual that might be termed a worship service. Once the person has reached the status of "clear" or "Operating Thetan," he/she is presumed to be superior and virtually super-human. Secrecy and isolation from those lower in the hierarchy, however, inhibit objective examination of this status (Stark & Bainbridge, 1980).

The Church of Scientology has had legal difficulties in Australia, Great Britain, with Interpol, and with several Federal agencies. On the other hand, its philosophies and practices have been introduced in schools both in Israel and the United States.

The Way International

The second largest cult in the United States is The Way International, founded by Victor Paul Wierwille in the early 1940's, when he claimed that God talked to him. A fundamentalist group, the Way has both communal residents and non-residential members, all of whom study the Bible and tenets of Christianity as Wierwille has interpreted them in his self-described role as a "spokesman for God" (Pogue, 1982). The principal activity for most members is attending daily Bible study classes either at one of the Way Colleges or at a Way "house" close to home. Those who live at the New Knoxville (Ohio) headquarters also translate Wierwille's books into other languages, do farm labor, and participate in various rituals. Recruiting is another major activity, with some being done at high schools where the teen-agers are urged to attend Bible study classes and go on weekend retreats. (They become full members at age 18.)

The Way is organized like a tree, with its trunk in New Knoxville, limbs in state-level organizations, branches in local communities, and leaves of individual followers. "Twigs" are home or communal study groups. New members are recruited at these study groups or fellowship meetings and are urged to pay $200 to take the "Power for Abundant Living" course — a series of videotaped recordings in which Wierwille teaches his interpretation of the Bible. One result of the course is that the individual is expected to speak in tongues, a Pentecostal practice (Conway & Siegelman, 1978).

The Children of God

The Children of God, originally founded as the "Teens for Christ" by David "Moses" Berg, and now known as the Family of Love, began as an evangelistic group in California in the late 1960's. Of the better-known cults, the Children of God/Family of Love is the only one to employ indiscriminate sexual relations exploitatively (known as "flirty fishing") in recruiting and fund-raising activities. (Although most of the "cults" are highly moralistic — almost Puritanical — in their views toward sex, both sexual abstinence and indiscriminate sexual relations avert the development of bonding between individuals that might compete with commitment to a cult and its leader.) Berg allegedly has demanded instant and complete obedience from his followers, although he denied this (Ericson & MacPherson, 1973). In his "Mo Letters," which are sold to raise funds, and "Pointers to Leaders," Berg repeatedly has urged the use of deception in activities from recruiting to public relations.

In its prime, the Children of God was like many of the other counter-culture groups in its antagonism to adults and "the Establishment." Despite Berg's orientation to Biblical fundamentalism, as he interprets it, he has made every effort to separate children from their parents and to destroy their individuality. Members live in small "colonies" subject to the direction and discipline of the colony "shepherd," bottom rungs of the group's hierarchy. They do not hold regular jobs, but sell their literature ("litnessing") and musical talents, charge admission to their discos, and require new members to sign over all their assets to the group to support the members.

A highly critical investigation of the group in 1974 by the Charity Frauds Bureau in New York State resulted in a shift to residence abroad by the leadership. Indeed, in the Ex-COG Newsletter, published by former members of the group, there are regular reports of overseas "colonies" and their activities. Members move about fairly frequently from the United States to Latin America, Europe, Canada, and Asia. There were, in the mid-1980's, several hundred "families" and well over 1000 children in the movement. The youngsters attend school irregularly at best, more often being taught at home when possible. Berg considers American schools to be not only godless, but anti-God and anti-Bible. He distributes his own views on child care and education which are followed closely by the faithful and lauded as being most beneficial to the children.

The Divine Light Mission

Another well-known cult is the Divine Light Mission, led by Guru Maharaj Ji. Its adherents stress the centrality of satsang (discourses on "the Knowledge"), service, and meditation as the rationale for the organization (Kemeny, 1979), but its opponents are disturbed by the total submission of members to the "perfect master," Guru

Maharaj Ji (Marin, 1979). The DLM encourages personal change in the individual as the way to ultimately transforming the world.

> Premies [followers] believe that Guru Maharaj Ji (like Christ, Buddha, and other great saints) is a living manifestation of the spirit and that he has come to bring peace to the world. They believe that the ego is the chief obstacle to peace and that surrender to Guru Maharaj Ji and to their inner spirit (God) is a necessary and vital step in the evolution of their consciousness and the salvation of mankind (Downton, 1980, pp.382-383).

Although drawn to the movement gradually, perhaps first through social contacts who were DLM members and who may have promised the experience of a "high" greater than from any drug, newcomers quickly become aware that as outsiders they do not have "the Knowledge." They can only obtain the Knowledge by conforming to the community and obeying the urgings of Guru Maharaj Ji to attend satsang and do service in the DLM's ashrams. This soon becomes a totally absorbing life-style and leads to the acceptance sought — conversion in the social and psychological sense and decreasing interaction with non-followers.

Recruits may live at home and work or attend college, or become part of a DLM ashram. Their absorption with DLM activities in every spare moment and surrender of will and critical thinking ability are elements that disturb their families and may ultimately disturb them if they defect from the Mission. Galanter and Buckley (1978) viewed DLM membership as a therapeutic experience for many as neurotic symptoms and drug/alcohol addictions disappear quickly after joining, but their view is questioned (see Chapter 5).

Common to these six cults and hundreds of others are the issues of recruiting and conversion techniques, vulnerability of recruits, and commitment which are controversial to some and alarming to others.

Patterns of conversion

Involuntary conversions were and are the most effective with those who are the most vulnerable — the young, the naive, the weak, and the neurotic. If young, these malleable individuals or victims are especially receptive to repetitive instruction, and, if chronologically and/or emotionally adolescent, they are also receptive to the firm guidelines and authoritative principles offered. In all such cases, they are easily "reformed" in a restrictive environment isolated from their families, and become convinced as converts of the errors of their former lives and beliefs. In the Mortara, Mallet-Bluth, Linneweil, and Cohen cases of the nineteenth century, and the Beekman, Finaly, and Friedlander cases of the twentieth, as well as in the cases of both Ratisbonnes, this pattern, perfected by today's "religious" cults, is apparent.

Sargant, a physician, likened some methods of religious conversion to modern political techniques of thought control (1957). He cited a number of techniques that have been used to modify normal brain functions for religious purposes. Meerloo (1956) also described regimens that could be used to heighten suggestibility and thus influence attitudes and behaviors. Several other psychiatrists (Lifton, 1961; Schein, Schein, & Barker, 1971) have described the thought reform methods used by the Chinese Communists during the Korean War, which are similar. The links among all these instances of conversion, religious or political, are evident when comparisons are made with a list of thought reform procedures given by Holt(1964):

1. Thought reform is *prolonged* - months or years

2. *Continuous* around the clock

3. Occurs in a *completely controlled environment* - no contrary information available

4. Social aspects of environmental control rob the prospective convert of his usual social supports and simultaneously subject him to massive pressures to conform to new beliefs and ways

5. Thought reform is *personalized*

6. Total *lack of privacy*

7. *Assault upon previous identity*

8. Systematic *application of rewards and punishments*

9. Sincerity, enthusiasm, and total commitment to the new idea(s) are demanded

10. All sources of resistance to the new ideology are exhausted

11. Active participation in "reforming" others is demanded

12. Synthesis and reconstruction - rebirth of a new identity (pp.295-298, italics Holt's)

In some cases, a step is modified in practice by one or another cult group, but in general, the conversion process in communal cults is essentially the same. The less highly structured cults use elements of this pattern, usually with emphasis on personalization, persistent persuasion, and social bonding.

Most of today's cults demonstrate the thought reform process in a highly refined state which is effective with some potential recruits with a rapidity appropriate to modern technology, even without the brutal physical punishment exercised by the Chinese. Bromley (1985) has asserted that if the techniques are effective, then recruitment should be high and defections low. To the contrary, he maintains, "New religious groups have remained small because of both their limited recruitment success and limited retention success. Defections begin soon after recruitment, and most members have left after two or three years" (p.14).

Although the absolute numbers of members may be small as Bromley suggests, and the estimates of numbers vary widely, the "limited success" in recruitment and retention is of small comfort to parents of those recruited. For the recruits themselves, even the time-limited affiliation can prove troublesome in later applying for a job or graduate school admission. If no information is provided for activities in that time period, the interviewer may make unwarranted assumptions about imprisonment or indolence; if "Unification Church" is listed, for example, or job skills learned and used in a cult setting are cited as experience, the interviewer may suspect the candidate's emotional stability (whether such suspicion is or is not justified). Therefore, the absolute numbers regarding success in recruitment and retention are less important than the long-term effects of the techniques used on those individuals who are recruited successfully (S.V.Levine, 1984).

The question of vulnerability

Hundreds, possibly thousands, of quasi-religious and
political cults have burst upon the American scene, and in
some cases the world scene, in the past two decades, actively
pursuing youths for the purpose of conversion. The number
of Jewish youths who have succumbed to their appeals is not
huge in absolute numbers, but it is disproportionately large
in terms of the percentage of Jews in the total population. Of
those events threatening the survival of the Jewish people —
intermarriage, assimilation, ignorance, antisemitism, and
proselytization — the last has intensified in recent years to an
alarming degree. What makes young Jews succumb? Why
are they apparently so vulnerable?

American Jews, since the end of World War II, have
become more secularized, more assimilated into the larger
society, more questioning of traditional beliefs and
behaviors. They tend to be a highly idealistic group, fighting
injustices against themselves and others. With non-Jews,
they have felt the negative impact of the rapid changes in the
post-war world. With non-Jews, as parents of today's youths
they have been confronted with conflicting theories of child-
rearing and of what their own goals should be. This has
often resulted in vacillating parental behaviors, which their
children condemn as hypocritical, and in weak emotional
foundations on which those children can base their own
lives. In general, the search for identity and purpose,
characteristic of the adolescent and early young adult
periods, has become more difficult and has led many youths
to rebel against their parents' life styles — to become
alienated from their parents.

Increased population mobility has reduced the influence of the extended family and even of local social institutions, with the result that more and more young people are drawn to their peer group for support and approval (Schwartz & Kaslow, 1981). Where no extant peer group provides fulfillment of the individual's needs for affiliation, acceptance, and empathy, the individual becomes more vulnerable to the proselytizers from both established churches and the cult groups. The impact of the social support provided can be seen, for example, in the assertion of 60% of Unification Church members that the support helped to "build relationships" that strengthened and expressed their religious faith (Kilbourne & Richardson, 1986).

Psychologists, psychiatrists, sociologists, clergy, and others agree that the vulnerable youths tend to be bright (usually attending or just graduating from college), of middle or upper-middle class backgrounds, in their late teens or early twenties, and lonely and idealistic. Beyond these common characteristics, investigators have variously suggested that cult recruits may be drug addicts who shift their dependence from drugs to the authority system of the cult (Simmonds, 1977a), or emotionally unstable (Galanter & Buckley, 1978), or seekers of religious truths (Cox, 1977), or individuals who have a weak relationship with their fathers and a lack of a sense of inner direction (Kaslow & Schwartz, 1983). Most of the recruits have had a minimal religious education and have few strong religious bonds. Indeed, E. Levine has pointed out that to his knowledge, there is no evidence from any source that "cult prospects give equally thoughtful consideration to the substance of their own religions, then balance the perceived strengths and weaknesses of their religions against those of the cults, and on this basis reach a decision whether or not to undergo conversion" (1985, pp.117-118). According to Stark and Bainbridge, "No matter what else may be required to produce a cult member, the process is greatly facilitated if a person has a problem, believes in the possibility of supernatural interpretations of that problem, and essentially is unchurched" (1980, p.1381).

Susceptibility is increased when young people are at a critical juncture in life: entering a new life situation (just after high school or college graduation; enrollment in a new college), after the break-up of a romance, during or just after exam periods. In some cases they are confronted with new people and/or new decisions to be made. In other instances, they may be lonely, depressed, rebellious, inexperienced at independent decision-making, and/or confused. In those few studies in which **former** cult members have been asked why they were attracted by recruiters' appeals, they reveal that idealism, the offer of a sense of purpose and commitment, and the opportunity to avoid feelings of loneliness were the dominant attractions. The religious ideology was not the primary factor, for indeed recruits were often unaware of the religious focus of the group in which they became enmeshed until a later time. By contrast, freshmen who were "able to achieve relative autonomy away from home yet maintain a comfortable relatedness with their parents had received [a] more consistent set of parental values" (Hankoff, 1979, p.206).

It might appear that involvement in a religious-type experience and with the total commitment provided by a cult is more desirable for those unable to cope with the problems cited than withdrawal into a schizophrenic state, drug addiction, or suicide Such an argument is weakened, however, except in the case of suicide, when one becomes aware of the need of many ex-cult members for extensive and intensive psychotherapy upon their extradition from a cult (Singer, 1979a).

Theodore and Alphonse Ratisbonne, as has been seen, both exemplify the vulnerable youth. Theodore was the lonely one, the searcher for answers to his questions about life, the believer that there might be a supernatural Being who could solve his problems. He was a "follower" until after his conversion, but had to be brought slowly to that decision. Alphonse, on the other hand, torn by his ambivalent feelings toward his forthcoming marriage, inwardly rebellious while outwardly conformist, and very peer-oriented, would have been easy prey for today's cult recruiters as he was for Theodore de Bussières. His conversion in a matter of days, even without the total isolation often found in the cult environment, parallels the modern recruit's experience. His knowledge of the Catholic religion to which he converted, like his knowledge of the Judaism that he abandoned, was minimal, just as the cult recruit today tends to have relatively little information about the commitment he is making and often a school-child's view of the faith in which he grew up.

That religion plays a minor role in today's conversions is seen in a study by Schwartz (1982). Among 48 ex-cult members surveyed, 38 said they had been coerced (but without physical force) into becoming a cult member. These same respondents cited the following reasons for young people being susceptible to cult recruiters (in order of magnitude): feelings of loneliness and/or alienation, a need for rules, a need for structure in their lives, an "inner weakness," lack of achievement, and some ten other reasons that were cited less frequently. The list is hardly surprising in view of the breakdown of traditional value systems during the past three decades as noted earlier.

The issue of informed choice

In all of the involuntary conversion cases of children included here, the principal figures were not informed of the commitments involved in their imminent conversion and therefore had no choice in the matter. Theodore Ratisbonne, after years of searching for answers to the questions that tormented him, did make an informed choice. Alphonse, to the contrary, experienced a "miraculous" conversion that he had not sought and would have opposed had he not been in so vulnerable a condition.

In the case of converts to today's cults, however, there is controversy about whether or not they have exercised informed choice with respect to conversion. Among writers sympathetic to the cults, the response, based on their investigations with in-cult members, is that there was not only informed choice, but also discussion about the impending decision with family and friends prior to joining the group (Shupe & Bromley, 1980). Other writers (notably Beckford, 1979; Greil & Rudy, 1981; and Schwartz & Zemel, 1980) are more cautious in accepting cult members' statements as entirely true. They aver that the statements reflect an attempt to reduce the cognitive dissonance aroused between reality and rationalization. This may be equally true for the statements of ex-cult members as well (Robbins, 1979).

Cult leaders, now more careful to have recruits sign consent forms when they stay with the group, aver that decisions to remain **are** voluntary and informed. Former members and investigative journalists, among others, assert that the choice made is frequently based upon incomplete information, provided under unusual circumstances. E. Levine has supported the latter view, asserting that, to the best of his knowledge, "there is no evidence from any source demonstrating that those who become cult converts are provided with all relevant and factual information (concerning cults' beliefs, practices, leaders' and members' ways of life) for their thorough examination and appraisal at leisure *prior* to conversion" (1985, p.117). The question of whether or not the decision to convert, or to join, is an informed one is thus a critical, and as yet unresolved, constitutional issue in the United States.

The initial contact with a prospect, either for solicitation of funds or for group membership, is often associated with welfare work for non-existent beneficiaries. "Front names" are frequently used by members of the Unification Church and other groups to disguise their primary affiliation, although there is increasing legal pressure on them to inform those they approach of their real identity. Both practices, however, commonly referred to as "heavenly deception," are acceptable to cults as being in the service of a "higher cause," that of acquiring converts and funds for the group. [Shupe and Bromley (1980) appear to justify such deception because of the financial "neediness" of cult movements (p.235).] Should the prospect ask probing questions of the recruiter or fund-raiser, the responses given tend to be vague and distorted bits of information, revealing as little as possible about the true nature of the group. It is doubtful, therefore, that the convert is aware of cult precepts and practices before making a full commitment. If this is indeed the case, then it would appear that proven deceptions constitute misrepresentation and/or fraud and are, accordingly, actionable in court despite First Amendment protection of the free exercise of religious choice (Schwartz & Zemel, 1980).

Although some cult figures have stated that their recruitment does not differ from that of nuns entering convent orders, Ebaugh (1977) and Bernstein (1979) have shown that the prospective nun, at least in modern times, is quite familiar with the theology of the Church and the life-style of nuns long before entering her novitiate. There is opportunity, even encouragement, for her to seek information about policies and practices of an order not only before entrance, but during the novitiate. There is freedom to leave the order if the novice, or even the professed nun, finds its life-style incompatible with her own philosophy. Although seclusion and eternal vows were characteristic of convents in the past, as we have shown, there have been many changes since Vatican II. As a result, the similarities between religious orders and today's cults lie in the use of thought reform processes to mold the newcomer into the new role (Ebaugh, 1977), obedience to authority, adoption of a new identity (although even that is changing to some extent), and commitment, but **not** in the area of informed choice.

Thought Reform

Holt (1964) indicated that the thought reform process was a prolonged one, lasting months or years. This is certainly evident in the children's cases examined, and in that of Theodore Ratisbonne. Edgardo Mortara, for example, was educated at the House of Catuchumens in Rome throughout the impressionable childhood and teen-age years. Joseph Coen's experience was very similar. Theodore Ratisbonne was subjected to proselytizing efforts for four years. The Bluth sisters were under the influence of Theodore Ratisbonne, Abbé Mallet, and other clergy for fourteen years, and Anneke Beekman was indoctrinated over an eighteen year period. By contrast, the youthful converts to today's cults are usually kept at training centers or as increasingly involved participants in cult groups for periods of a few weeks to a few months before themselves becoming missionaries for the group. However, indoctrination continues even after the commitment is made in order to reinforce the decision.

The goal clearly, in the Church and in the cult, is to have the individual not only conform and convert, but to commit himself or herself for life. The means to this end is a process of thought reform, also called "brainwashing," which includes extensive environmental and personal manipulation. [Conway and Siegelman (1982) have written that "brainwashing" cannot occur in the absence of physical coercion, but Meerloo (1956), Sargant (1957), and others cited earlier have indicated that this is not the case.] Harrigan (1979) has synthesized the process into what is almost a *pas de deux* between manipulator and prospective convert:

Reformer

produces stress by interrogation, threat, induced physical fatigue, and isolation from the familiar and supportive

exerts pressure to change by coercion, criticism, moral appeals, friendliness, repetition

Reformee

starts to succumb to individual and group pressure by reexamining beliefs and becoming self-critical

experiences conflicts of loyalty

feels guilty and anxious about beliefs and behavior

resolves self-image dissonance by confession and renunciation of past

Reformer

accepts confession if perceived as sincere

rewards by being genial toward reformee

reeducates

Reformee

finds self-realization in a new and meaningful life (p.18).

Thought reform **can** occur gradually, weaning the recruit slowly from one life-style to another. This pattern appears to be characteristic of those cults that are more committed to narcissistic than sociopolitical goals, such as the Church of Scientology and the Divine Light Mission, where members may live at home but spend their free time increasingly at meetings or training sessions. (There are instances as well, however, where a long-term commitment to these groups is made rapidly.) In some cases where members live in a communal residence, they may be in communication with their parents on mundane matters such as reassurance about their health and well-being, but more and more out of touch with their parents on matters of substance such as values, life-styles, and goals.

The differences in speed of effectiveness of thought reform techniques depends in part on those specific methods used by the various cults and in part on the degree of vulnerability of the individual recruit. Kemperman (1981), for example, vacillated for weeks until he decided to move into a "Moonie" residence. That led to an involvement that lasted more than three years. The ultimate effectiveness of the process, however, is similar for all of those who remain with a cult: conformity, commitment, and conversion.

Environmental manipulation

All of the writers on thought reform stress environmental manipulation as one of the essential elements in the conversion process. As we have seen, however, total environmental control is not uniformly the case. Where continuous supervision in a completely controlled environment, without access to contrary information, is practiced, the prospective convert is separated from his or her usual social supports — family, friends, and familiar life-style. This was obviously the situation in the children's cases discussed earlier and is also characteristic of some of the training centers of the Unification Church, ISKCON (the Hare Krishna Society), Children of God, and many other cult movements. Young people in these situations are not only the object of continuous supervision, but are also under continuing pressure to conform to the values and practices of the new community.

Approaches to prospective cult converts tend to be low-key and friendly, as the Mormon approach cogently demonstrates in their 13-step conversion program that literally begins with getting "a foot in the door" (Stark & Bainbridge, 1980). The "foot-in-the-door technique" requires the person approached to take some small action on a small scale, such as listening to the missionary's viewpoint. Freedman and Fraser (1966) found that it was then easier to have the person take a larger step in the desired direction than to have an individual with no previous commitment do so. Jim Jones made very effective use of this technique in the People's Temple, where "investment started off at a very low level, and gradually, almost imperceptibly, increased" (Weightman, 1981). Many of today's cults use much the same approach initially, inviting a youth to a friendly dinner or a lecture and later to a weekend stay. In most cases, the involvement then proceeds by small steps, almost as in Skinnerian linear programming, until the bonds between recruit and members are stronger than those between recruit and the outside world (Kemperman, 1981).

The cult member may offer assistance to a youth who looks lost or confused at transportation terminals or elsewhere (Edwards, 1979). The recruiter seizes that opening, and obtains a "foot in the door"; the conversation often ends with an invitation to meet the recruiter's friends who, with him or her, are involved in a "good cause." Proselytizers for "Jews for Jesus" groups often befriend newcomers to a college dormitory, and quickly extend an invitation to a picnic or other social function. If the prospect accepts the invitation, he/she is greeted by cult/group members with profuse expressions of acceptance and warmth, a technique known as "love-bombing." Divine Light Mission recruiters often use the experience of a grand emotional "high" from their meditation techniques as a lure.

At some point, the philosophy of the group is presented, usually in vague and high-sounding phrases that are sure to appeal to the idealism of the prospective recruit, but that actually reveal little about the true nature or goals of the group. If the group is part of the Messianic Jews movement, the emphasis may be on accepting Jesus as the Messiah while maintaining all the Jewish practices one cares to. The possibility of being accepted by the Gentile world without totally discarding Jewish roots evokes a positive response in youths who have found little fulfillment of their spiritual needs in institutionalized Judaism yet cannot deny their original faith. It is a bit more difficult to disguise the nature of a Hare Krishna group at an ashram because of their special dress and rituals centered on Krishna, but even here the totality of the commitment is not initially revealed. [Rochford's (1985) schedule for male members of one ashram strongly resembles the ritual-oriented day of contemplative monks, for example.]

Following the initial contact, the prospect is urged to remain or to return for another evening or to join these new friends for the weekend at a recreational site. The weekend ploy has been used extensively by some units of the Unification Church although other cults also employ it. The Way International, for example, sponsors weekend "retreats" or "Bible-study" sessions, although many of its members live at home full-time. The remote site offers the cult an opportunity to apply intense pressure for conversion in an encapsulated environment, such as Holt (1964) described, where there is no chance for consultation with family or friends about an impending decision or to reflect on what is happening. The "love-bombing" continues, with stimulation of guilt feelings if the recruit shows any signs of wanting to leave, or even shows reluctance to participate in the constant round of supervised activities.

Whether at an isolated site or in a communal residence, many of the cults provide a low-protein, high-starch diet, permit little sleep, allow no privacy, have a strict and exhausting daily routine, and subject the recruit to lengthy lectures filled with jargon. Such manipulation of sleep and diet leads to a heightened degree of susceptibility to suggestion according to Sargant (1957) and Meerloo (1956). As the recruit becomes more dependent on members' counsel and directions, more affected by the suggestions made, and more accepting of the group and its ideas, there is frequent positive reinforcement, usually in the form of abundant peer approval. The shaping of the recruit's behavior is effected with all the finesse of an expert in behavior modification (Stoner & Parke, 1977).

Part of the re-education process is the use of ritual and some kind of religious tone to impart the hope of personal salvation if the recruit joins the group. Motor acts, such as Alphonse Ratisbonne's writing a copy of the "Memorare" prayer, or the Hare Krishna member's daily active adornment of the Krishna figure, are often used to reinforce theoretical indoctrination. Chanting, recitation of a mantra, singing familiar songs with rewritten cult-oriented lyrics, and repetition of "religious" type phrases of greeting are some of the acts in this process. This was also a practice of the Father Divine movement of the 1930's (and later), for example, in what was almost a classic example of a cult, though less sophisticated and in some ways more constructive than those of today (Cantril & Sherif, 1938). The primary appeal is to the emotions, not the intellect. The chanting or similar activity, in fact, inhibits the use of the mind for other purposes, such as critical thinking.

Often fear of death or damnation is engendered if the recruit seems to reject what is offered. The family of origin is depicted as being an agent of the devil, thus weakening family bonds further. There is usually, however, a charismatic leader readily available to serve as an authoritative and authoritarian father-figure and to whom loyalty and affection can be transferred, such as Rev. Sun Myung Moon, Guru Maharaj Ji, David Berg, et al. (Rice, 1976).

If the recruit is subjected to a poor diet, little sleep, no opportunity to think for himself, lengthy boring lectures, separation from his family and friends, isolation from the outside world, and the prospect of doing arduous labor for very little in the way of creature comforts or material rewards, why does he become a member of the cult? Apart from being the object of very effective applications of conditioning techniques designed to change his attitudes and behavior, **his needs are fulfilled**. These needs are primarily those of affiliation and only secondarily religious. Stark and Bainbridge (1980), in their study of cult members, found that "In expressing interpersonal bonds as the prime factor keeping them in the cult, these members noticeably ignored the special qualities of the life-style, the religious exercises, or ideology" (p.1384). Kaslow and Schwartz (1983) similarly found that former cult members cited the acceptance and friendship of peers to be the greatest appeal of membership, and expressed feelings of guilt at having left their (new) friends behind when they left the cult. Perhaps S.V.Levine has most clearly expressed the drawing power of becoming a member of a new religion or cult. The affiliation, he asserts, does three things:

> First, a strong belief is engendered, a *raison d'être*, a seemingly coherent system of ideas and values. Second, and perhaps more importantly, is the rapid development of a sense of belonging, of communality, of being an integral part of a group which shares the members' feelings and aspirations. These two experiences — believing and belonging — serve to produce a third vital effect, a signficant increase in the individual's self-esteem. The result is a person with a strong sense of identity, feeling good about himself or herself, with a powerfully supportive group, and a shared ideology, affect, and catharsis (1979, p.594).

In the same vein, Pattison (1980) focused on personal social networks, some of which may be stress-producing, leading to or contributing to neuroses or psychoses. A normal social network, by contrast, is relatively small — 25 or 30 people — and provides social support, promotes good health, provides for psychic well-being, and often generates ethical norms. Pattison asserts that many of the religious cults attracting youths are similar to such normal networks. They are organized into small, functional units of around thirty people. They emphasize both affective and instrumental ties among the members. There is strong social support, with opportunities for frequent interaction. There are usually strong interdictions against drug use and the active promotion of healthful life styles. They generate strong ethical norms, built on explicit religious ideologies. And ... there are indications of salutary psychic improvement in the psychological adaptation of the devotees.

It is no wonder that the names used by these youth cults indicate the nature of their social structure: the Family of God, the Children of God, the Holy Family, etc. (Pattison, 1980, pp.283-284).

In the wake of the at least partial breakdown of normal family structure in our society in the past two to three decades, this viewpoint can be interpreted as valid. Clearly, it conveys a message to families about what is needed by young adults, and apparently wanted by many of them as well.

E. Levine has criticized fellow sociologists such as Anthony, Robbins, and Shupe because they

adamantly reject the body of knowledge dealing with human development, particularly the bio-psychologically established emotional needs of human beings. Nor do they take into account the psycho-social dynamics of the developmental processes that, from infancy into and through adolescence, so greatly influence ego and superego development, and thus the development of self-worth and self-confidence (1985, p.118).

Those cult members who achieve leadership positions and acceptance in the group are frequently gaining a measure of self-worth and self-confidence that they were not able to attain in the larger society. (Reluctance to lose such status is often a factor in the individual's decision to remain in the group, at least for a time, even when he/she has gained a more objective view of the group's goals and practices.)

Personal manipulation

Lifton (1961) has asserted that extensive personal manipulation follows environmental control. Personalizing the process incorporates assaults on the "victim's" previous identity in combination with the application of positive and negative reinforcement. Both in the initial contact between recruiter and prospect and during the early days of the "retreat" or stay in the communal environment, the prospect reveals, under astute questioning, enough details of his/her personal life that these can be employed in enticing him/her more deeply into the group. If such information includes, for example, tales of parent-child conflict or sibling rivalry, then the recruiter stresses the absence of such situations in the cult group, the "loving family" that now constantly surrounds the prospective member.

Part of the personal manipulation, according to Holt (1964), is a forced regression of the "victim" to childhood dependency. In addition to the techniques already mentioned, there is deliberate infantilization in some groups (as in having a new "friend" escort the prospect constantly, even to the bathroom), heterosexual (and homosexual) frustration, and evocation of feelings of shame and guilt. These feelings, crucial to the ultimate goal of destroying the prospect's identity in the process of creating a new one, may be aroused in children once they develop a super-ego, or at about four or five years of age. Also to be destroyed are

those elements of one's identity that appear by school age —
ties to family members, identification with an ethnic group,
and similar bonds, as well as personal standards of
achievement and behavior.

Study groups that require active participation and self-
criticism, but suppress negative comments or critical analysis
of cult philosophy and practices, help to break down the
individual's resistance. For example, if the prospect reveals
some minor personal flaw as part of the required self-
criticism and is hastily but thoroughly reassured by cult
members that they still love him/her, clearly this reinforces
the new bonds of affiliation and weakens those with figures
outside the cult who are perceived as less tolerant of flaws.
Peele and Brodsky, who studied the movement of addicts
and alcoholics to the cults, averred that "total commitment to
a religious sect negates everything that a person has been
and done and suffered and learned, and reconstructs his or
her thinking along the rigid lines of doctrinaire faith" (1975,
p.168).

Once the previous identity has been erased, the recruit
becomes as a new-born, perhaps even acquiring a new
birthday — the date on which the recruit accepted the new
faith. The Love Family, also known as the Church of
Armageddon, altered not only the birthdate but also the age
of its members. In some groups, part of the ritual of
assuming the new identity includes the acquisition of a new
name, as in several of the Eastern-oriented cults. Changes in
mode of dress, hair style, and daily habits as practiced in the
contemporary Hare Krishna movement, for instance, are
partly for the purpose of accentuating the birth of the new
identity (Daner, 1976).

Commitment

The ultimate goal of all these activities is total commitment to the new ideology. Demonstrable proof of the change from status of recruit to that of believer is seen in the new member's efforts to "reform" others. This last characteristic stage of the thought reform pattern explains the zealous proselytizing by the Ratisbonne brothers, the teachings of Canon Mortara, and even Anna Bluth's attempts to convert her family, as well as the recruiting efforts of cult members. Sontag, for example, in his study of the Unification Church, found that young people who joined were "willing to pour their commitment into a life of sacrifice and missionary zeal" (1977, p.209). "Hebrew Christians," Messianic Jews, and Jews for Jesus are similarly very active in trying to bring family and friends to their new beliefs.

Total commitment is total surrender to the authority as well as the ideology of the cult. In view of the gradual revelation of the latter, investigative evidence suggests that the former occurs first. From then on, the new member takes all pronouncements and actions on faith, faith that the leader knows best. The recruit, now a member in good standing, is relieved of all need to think independently or to make decisions. (This is one attraction of cult membership to many recruits.) Indeed, the Guru Maharaj Ji has openly advertised that followers should give him their brains. The implication was that they would have no further need to use their minds.

The sacrifices made, such as lack of independence, long hours of work and/or prayer, inadequate sleep, a non-nutritious diet, separation from family and friends of the earlier identity, and inhibition of the opportunity to mature in psychosocial development and in occupational or professional pursuits, are seen as clear evidence of devotion to the new leader, the new "family," and the new ideology. The ultimate reward for these sacrifices and for demonstrated ability in fund-raising and recruiting activities is advancement in the group's hierarchy. For many, abandoning the positions of prestige, success, and power attained in the cult to return to a "starting position" in the larger society is unthinkable, and therefore they remain with the cult for eight, ten, or more years.

Conclusion

The thought reform process is now completed. The vulnerable youth is informed at last of all to which he has committed himself, but his last independent decision was made far in advance of such knowledge in many cases. The time for decision-making, that formidable task that he may have been so reluctant to confront, is past. Extrication from his new life situation, should he become aware of inconsistencies or feelings of loss, is difficult. Vulnerability to appeals by members of the cult family to return to the fold should he leave voluntarily or be kidnapped and deprogrammed, continues to be high for some months after separation. If he rejoins the cult after being separated, the thought reform process, modified to fit the new situation, will be effectively employed again.

One might ask whether the fact that these new religious movements "have limited economic resources with which to initiate and sustain broadly based change" is adequate justification for tactics that "rely on pressure, deception, or public ignorance for their success?" (Shupe & Bromley, 1980, p.235). That is, do the ends, even if the group is legitimate and the convert is content, justify the means?

CHAPTER V — PSYCHOLOGICAL EFFECTS OF CONVERSION

Since religious conversion leads to a drastic change in the ideological system of the individual, there are concomitant inherent psychological effects on the convert as well. The acceptance of precepts often proscribed by the individual's original faith and adoption of attitudes and behaviors conforming to the new religion inevitably affect the convert's self-perception and perceptions of others. It is to these modifications that we now turn, for it is largely psychological needs that are being met by this singular act of altered commitment.

From seventy-five to two hundred years ago, conversion or re-commitment to religion represented a quest for and the fulfillment of future salvation, and an opportunity for acceptance in a rejecting and alien society by some Jews or other minority groups. Today we are witnessing a resurgence of the former trend among "born again" Christians, although the conversion of Jewish youth is directed more toward peer acceptance in non-traditional groups than toward Christian acceptance. To this latter group, particularly, conversion often is viewed as an experience that "can serve both to satisfy legitimate existential needs as well as to resolve personal intrapsychic and identity conflicts" (Levin & Zegans, 1947, p.81). Whatever the motive, however, conversion brings with it a "radical reorganization of identity, meaning, and life" (Travisano, 1970, p.600).

One must be cautious, however, in accepting the convert's version of what led to the conversion and what it has meant to him or her since. Taylor made the point succinctly, urging the researcher, and others, not to make the mistake of confusing retrospection with introspection (1978). Friedlander similarly indicated that

> An adult conversion may be purely a pro forma affair ... or it may be the result of a spiritual journey that ends in a decision freely made; nothing disappears, yet everything is transformed; the new identity then changes one's former existence into a prefiguration or a preparation (1979b, p.79).

Few studies have attended to this tendency to reconcile the pre-conversion life and the post-conversion ideology, although there are some available by a few sociologists, psychiatrists, and psychologists.

Shupe and Bromley (1980), Robbins and Anthony (1972), Damrell (1978), and Balch (1980) are among those who have attended workshops of the Unification Church or similar groups for research purposes. In their reports, it is stated that cult members were interviewed with the approval of the group's leaders and that therefore the samples may not have been random. These researchers overlook the fact that there is a difference between attending cult workshops or becoming a "member" of a group for research purposes and attending or joining as a naive young adult. Those who were recruited cannot be as objective as professionals doing research, and hence their reports about motives for conversion or the experience itself can only be regarded as biased.

Without pre-conversion data such as childhood/ adolescent diaries, anecdotal school records, and/or clinical test records, it is almost impossible to verify retrospective statements that attempt to resolve cognitive dissonance between the objective reality of pre-conversion needs and attitudes and the subjective perceptions altered by the new beliefs of what that earlier state was like (Beckford, 1978a, b,c; Kaslow & Schwartz, 1983; Singer, 1979a). Family photographs, too, would furnish objective views of familial relationships (Entin, 1982). The modifiability of recall of past personal behavior to be consistent with new attitudes has been demonstrated under laboratory conditions (Ross, McFarland, & Fletcher, 1981), though, as well as in the real world.

In his study of Jehovah's Witnesses, Beckford showed that "Witnesses internalize specific views of their organization and that these views are rationally used by them as resources when constructing their personal and collective experiences of religious conversion" (1978a, p.251). It is his contention, that there are, therefore, "severe problems in the conventional sociological practice of looking for individual converts' motives, predispositions, attractions, etcs., in their accounts of conversion" (p.261). Morton Prince similarly warned, years before, against trusting the narrative of the conversion experience itself, especially since it is "written from a religious and not from a psychological point of view" (1913, p.355). That there might be real disparities should be kept in mind as the statements of converts, independently or as part of research data, are examined. Rationalizations must be considered, even among the most sincere, for otherwise the convert might be revealed to himself or others as a dupe, indecisive, or worse.

Effects on the convert

The initial response to the conversion experience itself may be one of exaltation and joy, perhaps commingled with tears as we saw in the case of Alphonse Ratisbonne. A "sense of joy" or great happiness is a frequent descriptor of the immediate emotional reaction, sometimes accompanied by feelings of relief at having made and acted upon a momentous decision. More important than the initial reaction, however, is the lasting impact on the individual, if any, of conversion.

Historical examples

The long-term effects vary with the individual convert and his/her situation. Saul of Tarsus, for example, went from being actively opposed to Christianity to being equally active on behalf of it (Royse, 1904, p.145). The Ratisbonne brothers moved from passivity and religious non-commitment to being zealous proselytizers for their new faith. Moreover, Theodore, who had been especially passive, blossomed into an active teacher, writer, and charismatic leader (Isser & Schwartz, 1980). Alphonse raised money and founded a religious order in Palestine. Father Libermann founded a missionary society which served the needs of indigent blacks in Africa. Madeleine Semer discovered serenity and the ability to cope with personal unhappiness. Thérèse Martin, who also had a mystical religious experience, found happiness as a nun (Maitre, 1981). Edith Stein, a convert from orthodox Judaism to Catholicism before World War II, has been beatified by Pope John Paul II en route to sainthood (Rosen, 1987). Friedlander, an involuntary wartime convert in childhood, was, prior to being informed of his true identity, ready to follow in the steps of another involuntary convert, Edgardo Mortara, by studying for the priesthood (1979). The Finaly brothers, however, similarly converts to Catholicism as children during the Second World War and reconverted to Judaism in adolescence, appear to have developed little zeal for either faith (*Paris Soir*, 1978; Isser & Schwartz, 1980).

Some converts do experience a significant change in behaviors as a result of their new or strengthened commitment to religion. Nicholi (1974), for example, in a study of 17 Harvard and Radcliffe undergraduates who had had a "religious conversion" experience found that their post-conversion lifestyle and attitudes reflected several enduring changes. Because they now saw the body as a "temple of the Holy Spirit," they stopped using alcohol, drugs, and cigarettes. They also reported that their self-image had improved, that they had more positive feelings toward and improved relationships with others, and that they had renewed academic motivation, with about half changing career goals. As a group, they were also practicing more chastity and romantic fidelity as a result of adopting a new sexual morality in conjunction with the new faith. As in other studies of Christian converts (Allison, 1969; Paloutzian, Jackson, & Crandall, 1978), many of whom were "born again," there appears to be here a marked increase in purposefulness of life, religious orientation, social interest, and conservatism and/or dogmatism.

Theodore Ratisbonne, after a prolonged search for goals, an identity, and meaning to his life, made an intellectually-based conversion that not only changed his religion, attitudes, and activities, but also modified his personality markedly. In his extensive autobiographical writings, Theodore portrayed himself, throughout his pre-conversion period, as alienated and introverted. Dissatisfied with the roles he was to play as a member of a leading Jewish banking family, and unable to settle down intellectually, emotionally, or professionally, Theodore was not a very sociable person. After his conversion, he became an eloquent preacher, a productive scholar, and a charismatic leader (Isser & Schwartz, 1980a). Unexceptional as a student, he became pedantic in educating the girls entrusted to his care and also their teachers. Minimally committed to Judaism even when he directed the Jewish school in Strasbourg, he became an ardent proselytizer for Catholicism and a devoted servant of Mary.

His brother Alphonse, on the other hand, though similar to his older brother in terms of early lack of religiosity and post-conversion enthusiastic commitment, experienced less of a personality alteration. Unlike Theodore, Alphonse enjoyed the fellowship of his peers and the liveliness of Paris. As a priest, he continued to be gregarious (S.Carmelle, I, 1980), and found the rigorous scholarship and discipline of the Jesuits difficult to accept. The psychological effects on Alphonse were most marked immediately after his sudden conversion. Having had the highly emotional experience that he did, with attendant publicity, we conclude that he had to repress the doubts and conflicts that quickly arose as he realized what his new fervent commitment meant for his future.

The Bluth sisters, converted by Theodore Ratisbonne and his associates, and hidden for years with his help, endured varying reactions to their new status. Louise, apparently thoroughly intimidated by Abbés Ratisbonne and Mallet, followed their directives until she came of age, when she resisted their pressures to become a nun, and returned home (Isser, 1979, p.294). Elisabeth and Maria Siona (Anna), torn by their traumatic experiences while under the domination of the two clerics, became psychotic. Sophie, long secreted in several convents, and Minchen (Gabrielle) remained Catholics, with the former becoming a nun (Isser, 1979, p.295). These two, as a result of their conversions, gained new identities that separated and estranged them from their family.

Contemporary examples

Among converts to modern cults, the psychological effects may be diverse not only because of interpersonal differences, but also because of differences among the cults and among the researchers' orientations. If the researcher anticipates reductions in neurotic symptoms, he/she may unconsciously frame questions to elicit appropriate responses. If the researcher expects less drug use, that finding is almost assured, as very few of the cults permit drug use at all (sometimes not even allowing the use of medications). A similar risk exists when questioning former cult members who have been deprogrammed or who have had successful psychotherapy since re- or de-conversion. With those caveats in mind, we can recall also that those most susceptible to cult or missionary recruiting tend to be in conflict, depressed, or "at loose ends" — all problems that cult recruiters promise will be solved in the group.

Followers of "Bàba," an ex-New Yorker turned guru in his mid-thirties, perceived themselves as unconditionally accepted, relieved of guilt feelings by Baba's teachings, and with a new spiritual purpose in life (Deutsch, 1975). Both Deutsch and, earlier, Robbins (1969) who wrote about a guru named Meher Baba, noted that many of these gurus' adherents had been psychologically dependent on drugs prior to their conversion. The convert to Meher Baba's group in particular, who had formerly built an identity focused on the use of drugs, was now provided "with an alternative identity as a spiritual aspirant" (Robbins, 1969, p.312), and went "straight." As was noted in an earlier chapter, the alternative identity reflected a shift in dependence rather than a change from dependence to independence.

Galanter and Buckley found that converts to the Divine Light Mission (DLM) had a persisting "significant decline in the incidence of neurotic symptoms" (1978, p.685). Reduced use of alcohol and drugs, perceived positively by these researchers, was actually a result of the prohibition of their use in the DLM, and the reduced neurotic symptoms were a result, at least in part, of the total acceptance by and absence of decision-making pressures in the group. New identities were developed in the DLM, as in other Eastern-oriented groups, by the removal of prior identity symbols such as hair style, mode of dress, personal possessions, social associations, and even names (Daner, 1976; Downton, 1980; Enroth, 1977; Galanter & Buckley, 1978).

Converts in nine cults who were questioned by Levine and Slater (1976) reported that they found great comfort in the intense quality of belief experienced within their respective groups, the response to their existential questions. Unterleider and Wellisch, on the basis of two cases, reported new feelings of dominance among cult members or subjects who had been deprogrammed but returned to the cult anyway (1979b, p.280).

In a retrospective study of 40 ex-cultists, Schwartz (1983) found that 75% felt that the most attractive aspect of the cult to which they had belonged was the feeling of closeness and belonging and that 70% felt that the cult gave them a sense of purpose that had been absent in their normal family life. Even the experience of having been in a cult was not totally negative according to this sample, because since leaving the cult, they reported that they realized that they must take responsibility for leading their own lives and were more tolerant and understanding of their parents. Furthermore, to many the "formation of affective bonds within the group" provided enough spiritual support. The meaningful affective attachments solidify the conversion, enabling the subjects to separate themselves from their former associations with ease. Since the cult or the commune has become the focus of the individual's attention, it (the group) becomes the primary source of affective relationships (Greil & Rudy, 1981). Many young people in the 1970's, from nuclear divorced families, narcissistic, poorly disciplined, possessing weak or few internal standards, thus found in their peers more satisfaction and more emotional structure, enabling them to accept the charismatic leader and his theological beliefs and structures (S.V.Levine, 1984).

This element of support by the in-group network is particularly apparent in a follow-up study of 321 Unification Church members by Galanter (1986). In 1979, Rev.Moon chose spouses for this group, but marriages did not occur until three years later. Galanter found that, despite the "ample reasons for members to find compliance distressing, such as constraints on cohabitation and protracted departures to pursue church affairs, not to mention the fact that their spouses had been chosen by someone else," only five percent of the group left the Church (p.1248). He attributes this high retention rate to two principal factors: 1) "affiliative feelings [which] buffered them from disagreeable marital experiences", and 2) "The sense of good feeling associated with compliance [which] served as an operant reward for continued commitment and reinforced continued closeness to the sect and compliance with its expectations" (p.1248).

In almost all of the foregoing instances, the new commitment meant a radical change in theological affiliation as well as lifestyle and identity. Young Jews who became students at the yeshivot in Jerusalem, however, gradually deepened their commitment within the same faith. As a result, and in contrast to more classical forms of conversion, the *ba'ale teshuvah* experienced less conflict and more continuity with their pasts. "Unlike true converts, who often redefine their pre-conversion past as being undesirable and discontinuous with their new selves, *ba'ale teshuvah* see their transformation as a reaffirmation and realization of their true identities" (Glanz & Harrison, 1978, p. 137). Shaffir (1978) made the same point about the efforts of Lubavitcher Chassidim in encouraging greater observance of ritual among other Jews.

The enhanced self-perception found by Kaslow and Schwartz (1983) and Schwartz (1983) among ex-cult members is in marked contrast to the uncertainty expressed by ex-cult members in Beckford's sample (1978b). The divergence may be due to deprogramming and psychotherapy more frequently experienced by the American samples but not the British one. Other ex-cult members, however, have reported negative psychological effects of their deconversion and resumption of their original identity. Singer (1979) cited cases of former cult members who continued to experience periods of "floating," altered states of consciousness, and interference of cult jargon with their normal thought processes for several years, even with therapy. Feelings of humiliation at having been duped (Shapiro, 1977); and of guilt, both for their behavior toward their parents while in the cult and for abandoning their cult "family"; as well as fear of repercussions for their apostasy from the cult tend to persist among many of the former "converts" (Schwartz & Kaslow, 1981). These effects may be due, as Levine asserted, to

> The difficulties inherent in the process of leaving a closed, cohesive, presured, unidimensional social system, and being once again confronted by the very feelings which made one vulnerable to begin with — alienation, demoralization and low self-esteem — [which] are often more than the excultist can manage on his or her own (S.V.Levine, 1981, p.537).

West and Singer (1980), who have counseled several hundred ex-cultists, agree that the return from the totalistic environment where thoughts and behaviors are simply right or wrong to the larger society with its shades of grey, can exacerbate pre-cult difficulties or, at the very least, take several months for readjustment. Spero (1982, 1984) also noted that testing following the termination of therapy revealed better defense mechanisms and less rigidity of thinking than were apparent at the outset of therapy.

In a study of 66 former Unification Church members, Galanter (1983) found that they had better average "General Well-Being" scores two to six years after leaving the Church than either new recruits or active members. However,

> 36% of the respondents indicated the emergence of "serious emotional problems" at some time after leaving the church; 24% had "sought out professional help for emotional problems" after leaving; and 3% (i.e., two respondents) had been hospitalized for such problems during this interval (1983, p.985).

Conway and Siegelman, reporting on their survey of 400 ex-cult members, found that a large proportion of their respondents suffered periods of disorientation, relapses into meditation or chanting, nightmares, and "one in seven (14 percent) reported suffering from hallucinations or delusions for up to **eight years** after leaving the cult" (1982, p.90). These effects are attributed to the amount of time cult members spend in indoctrination and "mind control" rituals.

The American Psychiatric Association has categorized the type of behavior described by Conway and Siegelman, and other authors, as an Atypical Dissociative Disorder.

> This is a residual category to be used for individuals who appear to have a Dissociative Disorder but do not satisfy the criteria for a specific Dissociative Disorder. Examples include trance-like states, derealization unaccompanied by depersonalization, and those more prolonged dissociated states that may occur in persons who have been subjected to periods of prolonged and intense coercive persuasion (brainwashing, thought reform, and indoctrination while the captive of terrorists or cultists) (American Psychiatric Association, 1980, p.260). Such a description, of course, reinforces the view of Robbins and Anthony concerning the medicalization of the cult problem (1982).

There can also be positive effects for young people who survived the rigors of fund-raising forays and who rose to positions of responsibility within the cults. One former member of the Children of God/Family of Love, in addition to being more sensitive to the needs and difficulties of others, felt that she gained self-confidence as a result of learning to live in two other cultures and of surviving more than six years of difficult cult experiences (Hansen, 1982). She appears to be, however, from a number of pieces she has written, the type of person who consciously seeks out the positive aspects of events in an effort to use them constructively. It is hard to say whether this young woman is typical of ex-cult members. Several of her peers, however, have entered the fields of religion, counseling, and psychology after leaving the cults. They may represent a class of "survivors" who can overcome events rather than being overwhelmed by them.

Clearly, conversion or re-commitment does not occur without making some mark on the individual psychologically. Whether, as in most cases, he/she now perceives the self as a more desirable, possibly more "saintly" person, or experiences negative effects, there are changes in the person's attitudes and behaviors. There are, in addition, effects on the ways in which the convert perceives others.

The convert's perception of others

When the individual converts or becomes religiously more committed, not only is he/she changed in many ways, but the convert's views of and relationships with other people, in and out of the family, are also changed. Once converted, some newly perceive these figures from the pre-conversion past as sinners to be saved, as "creatures of Satan" to be avoided, or as unenlightened innocents to be proselytized. In other cases, of course, converts, from their point of view, take the stance that their choice has no effect on their perception of or relationship with others — although this subjective view may differ from objective reality.

If we look back at the nineteenth-century cases reviewed earlier, four of the converts altered their views of others as well as themselves. Edgardo Mortara, baptized as a child and educated with great care by the Church, came to see his family as ripe prospects for proselytization rather than the grief-stricken, loving parents and siblings that they were. When informed that the family had fallen on hard times as a result of trying to recover him, Edgardo did not respond at all. He felt it was God's will (Volli, 1960, p.38). After meeting with them in 1878, he continually tried, as a priest, to convert his mother and brothers to his adopted faith until one of his older brothers finally persuaded him to stop the effort (Volli, 1960, pp.39-41).

Anna (Maria Siona) Bluth was an active agent in the conversion of her father and siblings. She must have been quite persuasive and psychologically much stronger than her father to have been as successful as she was in this effort over several years' time. From her actions, it would seem that the converted Anna perceived her family as weak and unenlightened with regard to the "true faith" (Isser, 1979).

Strongly influenced by his spiritual mother-figure, Mlle. Humann, Theodore Ratisbonne adopted her special sphere of action — "salvation of the lost sheep of Israel" — as his own after his ordination (T. Ratisbonne, 1904, I, p.56).

Despite the fact that he had greatly embarrassed his family, Theodore urged them to convert as he had. When his father asked him if he was a Christian, soon after the conversion, Theodore not only responded that he was, but also that he was dedicated to the conversion of his "brothers," meaning all Jews (T. Ratisbonne, 1904, I, p.95). A letter written in 1843 contained his plans for an order dedicated to the conversion of Jews and for a school for the free education of Jewish girls, who would be baptized there (T. Ratisbonne, 1904, I, pp.318-319). Repeatedly, in letters and in personal contacts, it was obvious that the converted Theodore looked down on Jews as benighted, weak yet arrogant, hypocritical, and/or legitimate targets for his proselytizing activities. He thought nothing of deceiving families of his converts (T.Ratisbonne, 1904, I, pp.342-343, 572). Within his own family, however, Theodore (with Alphonse's help) was apparently successful in converting only one member — Edmond, son of Adolphe, the oldest Ratisbonne brother (T.Ratisbonne, 1904, I, p.600). Certainly his post-conversion perceptions of non-Catholics showed little charity or sensitivity to the feelings or beliefs of others.

The day after his miraculous conversion, Alphonse Ratisbonne wrote to his brother, Abbé Theodore, that if his fiancée Flore "does not have the strength to follow me, it will be necessary for me to renounce her ..." (Letter, S.Carmelle, I, 22 Jan. 1842). No regrets, no feeling of guilt about the possible renunciation of Flore, no sensitivity to the effects of his actions on her are to be found in the letter at all. (Clinically, this change in Alphonse, as well as the similar insensitive behavior of Theodore, would be viewed today as symptomatic of a narcissistic character disorder.) The conformity to his family's wishes that Alphonse had shown

154

earlier in Strasbourg was not demonstrated in Rome. Even his vague aspirations for the regeneration of Israel changed from the constructive plans for occupational rehabilitation of poor Jews to a more destructive program for the conversion of all Jews (Guitton, 1964, p. 115). This was his singleminded goal for the rest of his life, coloring his perceptions of family, Jews in general, and all others.

Modern Jews who have converted to "Hebrew Christianity" or "Jews for Jesus" groups are not only plagued by the "ineradicable" Jewishness within themselves, but frequently suffer as well from minority self-hate, often manifested in anti-semitic behavior. This is true also of Jewish members of several modern cults. The Unification Church, notably, blames the "Jewish nation" for the failure of Jesus' mission and considers that "The 'ignorance,' 'disbelief,' and 'stubbornness' of the Jewish people placed them 'on the side of Satan'" (Cunningham, et al., 1978, pp.114-115; c.f. Rudin, 1978, pp.76-77). Among the "Messengers," one Hebrew Christian group, "A corollary of the self-hate manifested ... is to be seen in the servile gratitude displayed toward Gentiles for any appreciation or acceptance they might manifest for the Hebrew Christian" (Sobel, 1974, p.105). They are also willing to practice deception in their attempts to win converts to their brand of Christianity (Gittelsohn, 1979; Juster, 1977; Lewis, 1979; Lustiger, 1979, p.34).

Cult members, whether converted emotionally or intellectually, are often taught that those not within or sympathetic to the group are therefore evil or Satanic. This alteration in perception of parents, siblings, and preconversion friends obviously affects any interaction with such outsiders. Ex-cult members have testified firmly to this aspect of their indoctrination (Enroth, 1977; Ericson & MacPherson, 1973; Gillis, 1976; Yamamoto, 1977), although such testimony is dismissed by Shupe and Bromley (1980) as merely another example of the "atrocity stories" told by deprogrammed ex-Moonies and other ex-cultists. [It should be noted that the "stories" told in the late 1970's reflect practices that have since been modified by some groups. Also, there appear to be differences between the post-cult experience reflections of "deprogrammed" ex-cult members and of voluntary defectors (Wright, 1984).]

The substitution of members of the cult as one's new "family" for the family of origin is a recognition by cult leaders of the need to belong to other people in an intimate, though non-sexual way. Moon and his wife are regarded as the "True Parents" by their followers. A similar arrangement has existed in the Alamo Christian Foundation headed by Tony and (the late) Susan Alamo. With the exception of Elizabeth Prophet, head of the Church Universal and Triumphant group, cult leaders either portray themselves as and/or are regarded as father figures by their followers, with their authoritarianism accepted in a way that the young person's father's was never accepted (Charity Frauds Bureau, 1974; Downton, 1979; Hopkins, 1969). The reaction of the discarded family members to these perceptions will be discussed later in this chapter.

In relation to non-family members, converts to the various cults tend to perceive other people as either sources of funds for the group and/or as prospective members. Much of the converts' time, in many cults, is therefore spent in the two activities of fund-raising and "witnessing." Nonmembers, being unenlightened and therefore unworthy of loving concern, are perceived solely as targets — more objects than humans in a sense. In addition, the time-consuming rituals and chores of most cults permit little time for maintaining normal outside social intercourse even if it were allowed. The emotional detachment from the outside world is reinforced for cult members by repetitive lectures in which they are told "Everything out there is frustration and loneliness; everything here is camaraderie and solidarity. You are helpless if you go back there" (Scharff, 1982, p.17).

It should be noted that ex-cult members tend to resume familial and social relationships that existed prior to their conversion. If a disharmonious family situation has not been resolved, however, such a relationship may be renewed on its original negative basis (e.g., parent-child conflict or absence of communication). If the latter is the case, the deconverted cult member may conclude that the cult leaders were correct in their view of parents and others, and may return willingly to the cult where the pressures are of a different kind and acceptance is a certainty.

Almost all of the published studies of converts and cult members have been focused on the convert "figure" and have omitted objective consideration of his/her background. However, the convert's commitment or conversion cannot be effectively understood without an examination of the context in which it occurred, and without a study of the effects of the conversion of those closest to the convert. When the convert's self-perception is altered there is, as we have shown, also a modification in the convert's perception of and behavior toward others. Therefore, in line with the principle that "for every action there is a reaction," we now will look at family reactions to the conversion of a family member.

The Family and the Convert

Like a pebble dropped into a quiet pool of water, the act of the individual radiates out in an ever-widening circle, influencing and affecting families, groups, religious bodies, and society in varying degrees. But there is always some effect, some reaction, however insignificant and imperceptible it may appear to be at the moment (Gordon, 1967, p.8).

The changes in the converts' beliefs and behaviors, attitudes and perceptions, have to have some effect on relations with family members. In some cases, the family is virtually destroyed as a social and psychological unit; in others, the family survives the immediate distress and is ultimately strengthened. Beyond the psychological effects, however, conversion has evoked legal action in many instances. The primacy of family rights has varied with jurisdiction and time, and remains a critical issue in the United States today as we shall see.

Effects of conversion on the family

The pebble dropped in Bologna in 1858 had an immediate and critical effect on the Mortara family, as well as ramifications to be considered later on the Jewish community and international affairs. The Mortaras, of course, immediately sought the return of their child. All pleas to the civil authorities and the Vatican were rejected. As part of its defense, the Vatican noted that, under a rule of Benedict XIV, the family could not claim that the baptism underlying the removal of Edgardo was invalid because it lacked witnesses (Volli, 1960, p.33). Nevertheless, they pursued every possible path to recover the boy.

Although Edgardo was ordained a priest in 1867 at the tender age of 16, members of his family continued their efforts. By rule of the Cardinal of the Inquisition, they had not been able to see him (nor had any other Jews) since his abduction. An attempt by his brother Ricardo to free him in September 1870 was not welcomed by the young priest. Marmalo Mortara, who had tried unsuccessfully for years to see his son, died of sorrow in 1871 (Volli, 1960, p.36). Edgardo did not meet his mother again until 1878, in Paris, some twenty years after being taken from the family. There was some contact thereafter, much of it a proselytizing effort on his part, but the persisting affection of the family for Edgardo was not reciprocated.

In the Mallet-Bluth case, the results were somewhat different. Here, the parents were divided in their response to their oldest daughter's conversion. The father, Jacob, accepted an invitation to stay with her mentor, Theodore Ratisbonne, in Paris, an invitation arranged by Anna, and was baptized, given communion, and confirmed within eight days (Isser, 1979, p.292). As a Catholic, he could no longer teach in a Hebrew school, of course. He subsequently sent for three other daughters and a son who he permitted, even encouraged, to convert. Meanwhile, the mother, Sarah Bluth, remained Jewish and sought to prevent the conversion of the three girls and another son. She fled to London with the younger children and obtained some support there from Jewish families and the Chief Rabbi. The three older converted children, Anna, Minchen, and Adolph, supported by Abbé Mallet and other churchmen, were at the same time prevailing upon the father to reassert his patriarchal rights (Isser, 1979, p.293). He was successful in this effort, and the entire reunited family moved to Cambrai.

When it became apparent that Abbé Mallet's relationship with Anna, Minchen, and Louise was licentious rather than clerical, the parents moved back to Paris. The father and Adolph abjured their conversions, and the parents began a long and painful campaign to have their other children returned to them from Catholic schools. The children were deeply loved, yet the family was almost destroyed in its attempts to give them independence while maintaining family relationships. When the case ended in 1861, there was no joyful reunion. Instead, the damage to the family unit, as in the Mortara case, was irreparable (Schwartz & Isser, 1979, p.353).

Elisabeth Linneweil's case was yet a third instance of overzealous proselytization and deception of her parents. Her father, once aware of the attempts to convert his daughter, searched for her continually while she was being moved from convent to convent. Although he had been content to allow others to raise her because of his travelling occupation, he was not prepared to renounce all family rights or to permit her to renounce Judaism. An impressionable young girl, Elisabeth had only sought to please those who had cared for her. Despite the pressures they placed on her, however, she was receptive to her father's wishes when she was, at last, reunited with him and made aware of his true feelings toward her (Isser, 1984).

As in the previous cases, the question of family rights became a matter for court action. Although French Jews had been emancipated earlier in the nineteenth century, the Church retained enough power to make it difficult for Jewish families to exercise their rights in these and other cases of conversion of youthful members. Evidently what was considered appropriate for Catholic families was not seen as appropriate for Jewish families.

When cases of child conversion arose almost a century later, following World War II, the position of the Church had changed and it joined civil authorities clearly on the side of familial rights. In April 1953, before the Finaly boys reappeared, Baudy wrote: "Is it not time for us to recall that the law is the sole authority in France, that no church has legal powers, that no sacraments of any religion have any civil validity? This has been the case for over a hundred and fifty years" (1953, p.557; c.f.Korn, 1958, p.173). The Finaly case, followed by the Beekman case, amply demonstrated that the Vatican would no longer support overzealous proselytization by individual laymen or clergy. In both instances, the parents of the young converts were killed by the Nazis and could not protest the abduction and conversion of their children. For the Finaly brothers, there were surviving aunts who sought their custody; for Anneke Beekman, the battle was fought by the Jewish community.

In the Finaly case, their aunt, Mrs. Fischel, was to become guardian of the boys if their parents did not survive the war. Mlle. Brun, their temporary custodian, wrote to Mrs. Fischel in November 1945 that the boys were still Jews and that she wished to continue to care for them. Mlle. Brun, at the same time, had herself declared their guardian through the device of a legally-appointed "family" council (which did not include any family members). Why neither Mrs. Fischel nor another aunt, Mrs. Rosner, did not take legal steps at that time is not known, but this may have been related to the unsettled state of affairs in Europe following the war. Although some correspondence did ensue, Mlle. Brun had the boys baptized in 1948; the family sued for their recovery, also using the family council device. In late 1949, a French court ordered Mlle. Brun to surrender Robert and Gerard to Mrs. Rosner, who lived in Israel. For four years, the Rosners pressed their case, wanting very much to raise their nephews as the parents had wanted. They even agreed, as part of the case settlement, to allow the boys to attend mass if they could only have them in Israel.

Once in Israel, in mid-1953, the young brothers did go to church for a time, having been strongly influenced by their rigorous Catholic upbringing. However, as the Rosners may have foreseen, interaction with Israeli peers gradually weaned them from Catholicism and they adopted Jewish beliefs and cultural values. The love and warmth of their new-found family, and apparently gentle handling in the area of religion by the Rosners, led to a voluntary de-conversion that has persisted into adulthood (Schwartz & Isser, 1981).

For Anneke Beekman, successfully hidden in convents until she reached 21, there was no family to draw her back to Judaism. Once she was an adult, the choice of religion was legally hers despite the earlier communal protests. For Saul Friedlander, who also had no surviving family, the honesty of a respected priest provided new options and he chose to live with a warm and supportive Jewish foster family. His de-conversion, like that of the Finalys, was voluntary. The question of familial rights for these four individuals arose only because the conversion events occurred when they were minors.

In the case of the Ratisbonne brothers, familial rights were moral rather than legal as they were adults at the time of their conversions. Their father wept when Theodore admitted his conversion, and he could not speak for several minutes. Finally, the father said that this was the worst and most irreparable of the evils in his life, and that he was happy that Theodore's mother had died before witnessing this affliction (T.Ratisbonne, 1904, I, p.95). He cursed his son for his apostasy and conversion. According to Theodore, they were reconciled on the condition that he cease teaching at the Jewish school. Not too long after, however, he wrote a prize-winning essay on the elements of a moral education, the conclusion of which strongly favored a Christian education. Theodore had the insensitivity to dedicate the work to his father (T.Ratisbonne, 1904, I, pp.99-101).

In Alphonse's recapitulation of his own conversion, he included comments on Theodore's conversion and its effects on the family:

> About the year 1825, an event occurred which caused my family deep affliction; my brother Theodore, on whom their chief hopes were founded, embraced the Christian religion, and shortly after, notwithstanding the most pressing solicitations, and the affliction he had caused, he went a step further; — he became a priest, exercising his ministry in his native town, and under the very eyes of my inconsolable family (A.Ratisbonne, 1842, p.9).

Alphonse remained estranged from Theodore, with the exception of some minor formal correspondence, until the day after his own conversion. For Alphonse, anger at his brother was an expression of what Bowlby calls the first phase of mourning (1961, p.333), since this was a loss of yet another member of his family.

By the time Alphonse converted in 1842, his father had died, and was thus spared a second such shock. His uncle, however, sent one of Alphonse's brothers to Rome immediately in hopes of persuading the convert to recant before he was baptized. According to Theodore, the brother who had been dispatched to Rome, wounded to the core, said that Alphonse "became the assassin of his uncle and his fiancée" (T. Ratisbonne, 1904, I, p.233). In March 1842, the family wrote Alphonse asking that he return to Paris promptly so that the family could resolve his situation (T. Ratisbonne, 1904, I, p.245), but he refused. He did, however, maintain some relationship with those sisters closest to him in age. He wrote to them for money from Jerusalem, after he had established a chapter house there, supposedly because he was in ill-health. When they sent funds, though, he used them to support his missionary activities. The estrangement from other family members apparently continued until Alphonse's death.

Other adult conversions have brought similar negative responses on the part of families. There is a basic feeling, even when the family is not religiously observant, that the family has been rejected. However, where the family follows orthodox Jewish practices, their rejection of the convert is total, with mourning rites observed as if the apostate were dead. This extreme response is not limited to Jews, though.

In families known to one or both authors, Catholic families have similarly cast off children who converted to Judaism, or, in a few cases, were romantically involved with Jews. (Such a break is not restricted to the major faiths. The Amish and Jehovah's Witnesses, for example, shun — or totally avoid — apostates.) Despite the total rejection by the family, there may be limited contact between some family members and the convert as time passes, particularly where severe illness occurs or grandchildren arrive.

Less religiously observant families may not mourn the convert as if dead, but they do experience feelings of shock, anger, rejection, guilt, and shame. The anger and rejection are directed at the convert, the guilt at themselves, and the shame in their relations with the extended family and the community. In addition,

> The parents of Messianic Jews are appalled at their children's decisions. Many feel that six million Jews died in the name of Jesus Christ; now their children are claiming to follow the religion of their murderers. While some Jewish parents do try to understand and not press their children out of their family fellowship, many disinherit and sever themselves from their children (Rausch, 1979, p.37).

Rejection responses may range from banishment from the home to temporary estrangement, but the anger tends to emerge and persist both in direct confrontation with the convert and in discussions with others. (For a fundamentalist Christian response, see L. Cox, 1986.)

Parents of both "Jews for Jesus" converts and cult members, if uninformed as to the true nature of their children's new affiliations, may initially treat the news of new-found friends casually or even with pleasure. The temporary withdrawal from college, if that occurs, is perceived as a phase that will quickly expire. If the youth has previously been involved with drugs, the parents may view membership in a "religious" group as beneficial. As time passes with less contact from the child, however, or as the parents become more aware of the nature of the group, they respond with alarm and anguish. They cannot understand why their child has punished them in this way, what they did to "deserve" such unfilial behavior. Disbelief, anger, depression, sadness, and hopelessness dominate the family's reactions. "Someone they care about has disappeared, often without warning or without giving the parents an opportunity to try to work through the kinds of longstanding problems with their youngster that contributed to his/her vulnerability to the beckoning, warm welcome of the cult" (Schwartz & Kaslow, 1981).

One parent of a Unification Church recruit reflected further on his mystification: "How could any religion that as its first consideration tries to break the biological bond between child and parents be good? How can they pose as Christian, when they reject one of the commandments that underpins the Judeo-Christian philosophy: 'Honor thy father and thy mother'" (Adler, 1978, p.28). Most parents of cult members, confronted with their children's dedication to anything that calls for a break of family ties, charge the cults with brainwashing (Belford, 1977, p.337). Before they reach that point, however, they may scream imprecations at the youth, revile the cult, and make threats that they will not or cannot carry out. Such behavior only exacerbates the situation. When it proves ineffective in regaining the "lost" youth, the family seeks other courses of action.

In a survey of ex-cult members and their parents, almost all of the 58 parents indicated that they had initially been confused, depressed, angered, and at a loss when they first became aware of their children's involvement with a cult (Schwartz, 1983, 1986). In most cases, however, they sought information on the groups, help from professionals (clergy, physicians, social workers, et al.) in the community, and ultimately both information and help from parents who had already experienced a similar trauma. Far from berating their children, they attempted to maintain communication with them, not always successfully, through letters and phone calls. Some went so far in this attempt as to attend meetings of The Way International, Divine Light Mission, and ISKCON (Hare Krishna movement).

One group of parents shares some of the confusion and stress that afflicts the parents of cult members, yet also experiences feelings of ambivalence. These are the parents of youths joining the Jewish "counter-culture," making aliyah (immigration to Israel), enlisting in a Chassidic movement, or enrolling in a yeshivah, making an alternation of identity *a la* Travisano (1970) rather than altering their identity. Rabbis, Jewish educators, and community leaders preach the virtue of such moves, usually supported in theory by parents — but for someone else's children. When theory becomes practice for one's own children, the parents are almost as distressed as if they had joined a Hare Krishna ashram. [For many months in 1982 and 1983, a small advertisement appeared in the "Personals" column of the Sunday edition of *The New York Times*. It was addressed to parents of youths who had joined with the Lubavitcher Chassidim and obviously sought to form a parent network and support group.] Their feelings of being criticized and rejected for their values and practices is almost the same. They question why their children cannot continue in the secularized pattern the family follows, and often perceive the imposition of kashruth (keeping a kosher home) and change in appearance as unmerited burdens. Yet, while "parents may not be altogether happy about their son's shift to Orthodox Judaism, they cannot honestly view it as an act of betrayal or a failure. If anything, they appear to feel that they 'succeeded only too well' in raising their sons as committed Jews" (Glanz & Harrison, 1978, p.123; c.f. Warshaw, 1979, p.108). The same obviously holds true for daughters as well who become affiliated with an orthodox group independently or through marriage, and for Jews in Israel as well as in the United States.

Courses of action

When a youth converts to another faith or joins a cult, there are only a few directions in which to turn. Many parents go first to their clergyman. If the rabbi or minister knows little about cults, his/her counsel may be simply to pray harder, or may encourage disengaging from the child until he or she "repents." A more knowledgeable clergman will help the parents to face their feelings, give them information, and direct them to community resource agencies or support groups. (Note: The community responses will be discussed in Chapter 6.)

A second path leads to other parents who have had the same experience. Here the distressed parents have the opportunity for mutual commiseration, but more importantly, learn how to deal with the absent youth and how to seek his/her return effectively. Sometimes the support groups are under the aegis of Jewish community agencies; sometimes they are independent and non-sectarian. In either case, the parents become aware that they are not totally guilty in the situation, that their initial responses were normal, and that they should maintain communication with their child whenever possible. They may also receive advice about the pro's and con's of hiring a deprogrammer or of attempting to kidnap the youth themselves.

Another professional often consulted by distraught parents is an attorney, in hopes that there are legal avenues through which the cult member can be recovered. There are several obstacles facing the parents here: 1) if the absent child is 18 or over, he/she is legally an adult and therefore free to choose a religion independently of the parents; 2) few attorneys have had experience in dealing with such religious issues, especially against seasoned ACLU and cult group attorneys; 3) cults, claiming to be religions, are protected under the First Amendment; and 4) proving that the youth has been subjected to psychological and/or physical harm is very difficult, especially if parents bring the suit (Schwartz & Zemel, 1980). Class action suits have been brought by groups of parents, but the results so far have been inconclusive because of variations in state laws, the grounds on which the suit is based, and the leanings of the judiciary.

At some point, many of the parents turn to psychotherapists in an attempt to sort out their feelings. Even these professionals, however, are not uniformly aware of the cults or of how to provide the needed emotional support. Where psychologists or psychiatrists are knowledgeable, they can focus on problems in the family, conceptualizing the cult member as the identified patient or scapegoat, and helping the parents understand the family dynamics and structure. In this way, during the period of waiting for the child to leave the cult or be removed from it, the parents and their other children can be helped to function in a healthier fashion (Schwartz & Kaslow, 1981).

When and if the young adult returns home, many families have found that continuation in therapy has been beneficial to the ex-cult member as well as other family members in the readjustment of all concerned (Schwartz, 1982).

Counter-conversion

Whether the young person's conversion was to another religion or to a cult, de-conversion is difficult. Once the rupture has occurred in a family, it can be mended, but the family will rarely be the same as it had been earlier. (Can you picture the Ratisbonnes if Theodore and Alphonse had recanted?) For the youth, he or she often finds that "one can't go home again," at least not as if there had never been a departure (Travisano, 1970, p.596). For the family, there is an analogy to other catastrophic situations. When a family member has attempted suicide, for example, the rest of the family regards that individual differently thereafter. There is a chronic anxiety about another attempt at total flight. Further, if word of the attempt has spread, orally or in print, can the individual face others without embarrassment, feelings of guilt, and rationalizations — much the same as a religious convert or cult member who seeks to de- or re-convert? The difficulty is similar, and probably more trying the older one is, to admit being "taken in," or behaving impulsively or irrationally.

Shupe and Bromley (1980) have made a number of anti-parent and anti-middle-class-values statements in their book on the anti-cult movement (see especially pp.37-42, 152, 170, 190-192). When there is an affectionate bond, however weakly expressed, and when there are psychological ties based on roughly two decades of living together as a family, it seems difficult to justify such criticism. What is so bad about parents caring about their children, even as adults, or trying to transmit values to them? The latter has been a traditional role of parents in society for centuries. Indeed, as noted earlier in analyses of the roots of the cult phenomenon, one of the causes of youthful disarray today has allegedly been the unwillingness or inability of parents to fulfill this traditional task of transmitting values. Melton and Moore (1982), theologians who tend to be supportive of alternative religious patterns, concede that even where the group's practices are relatively benign, the family's distress is understandable and they offer sensible guidelines toward the relief of such distress (pp.97-123).

Similarly, conversion to other faiths has frequently been blamed on parents. It is alleged that they have not communicated religious principles and practices either through conscious teaching or by example in their own lives. Whether or not parents are largely at fault (and many would assert they are not), they cannot combat proselytization by churches, ardent missionaries, or cults alone. From the Mortara case onward, they have had varying levels of Jewish communal support. In the next chapter, the quantity and quality of that effort is examined.

CHAPTER VI — COMMUNITY RESPONSES TO
PROSELYTIZATION

The proselytization efforts of various cults and evangelical sects have presented a threat to the community, for the family's well-being is essential to the stability and continuity of the group. Institutions such as the school, the church and synagogue, the club have traditionally been the arbiters of values, of training, of standards, and indeed have been the shapers of the entire social fabric. Conversion, therefore, involves nonconformity, rejection, and even desertion of the group and its established norms. Large scale defections, by young adults in particular, have long been regarded with suspicion, distrust, and anger. Often, intercommunal conflicts have resulted because of bad taste, insensitivity, or dishonesty on the part of the missionaries. But even more often, these animosities were also the recognition by the community of the dangers to its survival presaged by successful proselytization. Presently, mainstream Christian groups are upset and even resentful of many of the cults' activities (c.f. Vatican Secretariat, 1986), although in self-interest they must oppose anti-cult legislation that might weaken First Amendment protection of all religions. They, too, deplore those recruitment methods which smack of deception and manipulation. However, the most anxious and the most apprehensive of all communities are the Jews.

Historically, the memories of forced conversion, religious persecution, and finally the Holocaust remain potent. The sufferings caused by expulsion from various countries, from the thirteenth through the sixteenth centuries, were only minimally relieved by the growing movements toward human freedom and dignity two centuries later, especially for those who did not joyously and gratefully seek to become assimilated. Salo Baron pointed out that the negative attitudes encountered by Jews throughout the centuries were based on a "dislike for the unlike" (Baron, 1976). "unlikeness," or difference, has been shown to provoke feelings of anxiety, jealousy, and even of guilt, that contribute to negative attitudes and behaviors. Moreover, the nature of Christianity, with its exclusive claim of salvation, gave an impetus to and justification for the continuing struggle to save souls, particularly Jewish ones, that continues, as we have shown, at present. The English Missions to the Jews of the nineteenth century (Scult, 1973) have their equivalents in the "Jews for Jesus" movements today, as well as in the more traditional evangelical missions that call for a return to a "Christian" America (Briggs, 1980).

The "Jews for Jesus" movement is a lineal descendant of the nineteenth century missions in England and America directed towards the Jews. Earlier, "Hebrew Christians" was the name assumed by these groups, and, as the present-day members do, they, too, maintained Churches for their compatriots. Formerly, the term "Hebrew Christian churches" referred to those congregations of converted Jews who were to maintain their Jewish identity within the church. The segregation reflected the unwillingness of the Christian community to totally absorb and assimilate their converts.

On the other hand, the "Jews for Jesus" movement springing out of this historical precedent has developed new and entirely different characteristics. Unlike earlier converts, "Jews for Jesus" wish to maintain their ethnic roots. They desire to proclaim their Jewishness, and yet accept the Christian belief system by proclaiming, as earlier missionaries did, that Jesus represents the ultimate completion of Judaism. Again, unlike earlier converts, they eschew the denunciation of Jewish teaching and ritual. They use the Sabbath, the music, and other traditional symbols to entice Jewish youth. What makes them despised by the Jewish community is that they attempt to sell Jews the idea that they can accept Christian teaching and still remain practicing, presumably devout Jews; that young Jews can go to a Christian church using Jewish symbols and that they would not tear asunder the bonds that tie them to family and community. Their teaching is plainly fallacious, insensitive, and too, often strident and aggressive.

Their appeal is also based on historical lessons. Many Jews who showed a preference for Catholicism, such as Franz Werfel or Henri Bergson, were reluctant to convert formally because they did not wish to sever completely their communal bonds. In contrast, a very large number of American Jews were attracted to and even accepted Unitarian Christianity, Christian Science, or Ethical Culture. They hoped to achieve religious acculturation, or to engage in a more satisfying spiritual transition. However, in these sects or denominations, they were not obliged to accept Jesus as their messiah or as a divine figure. In essence, these Jews did not renounce their past. The leadership of the present "Jews for Jesus" movement has attempted to reconcile traditional Judaism with Christianity in a way that they hope

can recreate a pattern similar to the one that Ethical Culture
used. The difference is marked. Ethnicity has been more
popular in the 1970's and 1980's than half a century earlier,
and religious acculturation is less desired. Their emphasis
on tradition becomes, therefore, a means of enticing Jewish
youth to accept essential Christian truths cloaked in Jewish
wrappings.

Although religious prejudice has varied from country to
country, one fact remains the same. Many Christians
regarded (and still regard) Judaism as a source for potential
converts, and Judaism as a "not quite equal" or a "fossilized"
religion (Toynbee, 1947). The nineteenth and twentieth
century cases focused upon in this volume, although
dissimilar in many ways, reveal this attitude quite clearly.
The effects of conversion on the individuals and families
involved have already been examined. The ways in which
the Jewish community has reacted to these events are a
critical part of the total picture.

Community Response

The first case at issue was the Mortara Affair, which
aroused enormous controversy and produced, for the first
time, widespread international cooperation. The case
illustrated to Jews their new problems and continuing
precarious status, despite their acquisition of civil freedom.
The triumph of emancipation and assimilation in the
nineteenth century posed a new challenge to the Jewish
community — that of survival. The reaction of the Jews
reflected their awareness of these threats. In 1858, the Jewish
community, first in Sardinia-Piedmont and then throughout
Western Europe and the United States, reacted to the

Mortara case in a positive fashion to protect itself from what it considered dangerous enemies. Despite variations in lifestyle and communal animosities which existed in the Diaspora, they perceived correctly that they were threatened by the actions and political beliefs of the Church. Hence, they closed ranks in the face of direct danger to their co-religionists and indirect danger to themselves.

Twenty-one Sardinian congregations addressed an appeal to the London Board of Deputies, representing English Jews, and to the French Central Consistory. Their petition urged that Jews make their voices heard in protest of the Papal action (London *Jewish Chronicle*, September 10, 1858). As a result, Jewish, as well as world, opinion was mobilized and expressed its outrage in an angry barrage of editorials and petitions to persuade the Papacy to alter its decision. Jews in the United States, France, Holland, Prussia, and England cooperated in seeking redress for the Mortara family. Despite all attempts by individuals, communal groups, the French government, and the media, however, Edgardo Mortara remained with the Church for the rest of his life.

Nevertheless, the publicity surrounding the Mortara Affair had considerable significance. It aroused Jewish communities to unite within and with each other for defensive purposes, a move assertive and innovative for its time. The desire for concerted activity led to the formation of the Alliance Israelite Universelle and other similar organizations to protect Jewish interests throughout the world. This cooperation had tentatively been attempted during the Damascus Affair in 1841.[1] The Mortara Affair again galvanized Jewish communities into pursuing political aims, an activity that has continued into the twentieth century.

This reflected a change in community behavior from passive adaptation to active self-protection. This feeling of inter-dependence and the sense of mutual responsibility among Jews has been essential for their survival as a people, whether the crisis concerns one individual, as in the Mortara case, or a whole country, as in the instance of Israel's 1967 and 1973 wars. As Lewin has pointed out, this factor of dynamic interdependence is critical to the concept of a group (Lewin, 1951; c.f. Herman, 1977). Community action groups have persisted from the mid-nineteenth century to the present; united action, however, has had to be generated anew as new crises have arisen for individual Jewish communities or for all of them.

As Jews joined the mainstream of economic, social, and political life in their respective Western nations in the

---

[1] In 1840 the death of a priest in the city of Damascus aroused the old charges of ritual murder against the Jews. This led to the persecution of Jews. Leaders of the French and British Jews (Sir Moses Montefiore, Adolph Crémieux, and S. Munk) went to Egypt and petitioned Mohamet Ali to rectify these injustices. They were successful.

nineteenth century, assimilation seemed to be almost complete. The ethnic dimension of Jewish life diminished as Jews adapted to the culture, while acquiring characteristics of their new national identities. There were symptoms, nevertheless, that indicated that their communities remained cohesive and identifiable. Occupationally, for example, Jews tended to remain urban and continued to focus on certain businesses, trades, and professions — remaining easily visible. On the other hand, their children were often tempted by the seductions and promises of the majority religion, as we have seen, and the social gains it promised through conversion. Furthermore, the Jewish community itself was a direct target of continuing missionary activity, either Catholic or Protestant as we have already shown. Intermarriage, even then, also posed a problem, as it continues to do today.

Even more insidious and widespread, and an enemy of other faiths as well, was the prevailing secularism embraced by innumerable Jews. This further vitiated the intellectual and religious vigor of Jewish communal life. Jewish educational institutions were weakened, and the use of Yiddish was discouraged. This was seen clearly in the readiness of Jewish parents, such as the Bluths, to send their children to Catholic schools, or the family of Alphonse Ratisbonne to send him to an exclusive Protestant school.

Finally recognizing the dangers, community leaders set out to combat these polycentric tendencies which seemed likely to annihilate the remnants of common identity. In this group effort, as Freud pointed out, men's emotions were exalted and intensified as they could not be on an individual basis (Freud, 1922/1959). These emotional reactions gave impetus to the creation of institutions to perpetuate Jewish culture and to meet the community's special needs: schools, newspapers, and charitable institutions.

Theodore, as noted earlier, was teaching in such a Jewish school at the time of his conversion. Some twenty-five years later when he had already begun his own school for the education and conversion of Jewish girls, he was extremely irritated by the resistance of the resurgent Jewish communities:

> The synagogue, at this time, showed itself more and more resolved to paralyze Christian proselytizing. To succeed, it had to work to create schools which, undertaken by rich Jews, attracted the children of their poor coreligionists. They wanted to facilitate and generalize the instruction for which all were avid, and which, without special institutions, they had inevitably requested and received elsewhere. Their classes were quickly filled because, swayed by the pressure of almost unconquerable prejudices, were added the fear of irritations reserved to those whose free choice had carried them toward Christian teachings. The refuges and entrances to the neophyte state declined in proportion. Nevertheless, the past results obtained guaranteed the Daughters of Zion that which they had a right to hope for again (T.Ratisbonne, 1904, I, pp.590-591).

The Jewish community had already been incensed by his activities, especially by his death-bed conversions of several Jews, and protests had been lodged with the French government in 1841 by the Central Israelite Consistory. Ratisbonne exploded angrily at the Jews, irritated by their "persistence in maintaining the religious debris of Judaism ..." He assailed Protestants as well, accusing them of being "religious speculators or Bible distributors." As a witness at the trial of Canon Mallet in 1861, he received widespread notoriety for his part in the Bluth girls' kidnappings. The Jewish press castigated him roundly saying:

> These apostates from the paternal faith, these deserters from the sacred militia, these traitors to the God of Israel: We see them quitting our ranks and going over to the enemy, who outwardly receives them with cries of joy, but inwardly despises them. We also know the various motives which actuate them... With none of them, is it conviction. What they wish is to satisfy their ambitions and passions (*Verité Israelite*).

The French anticlerical press also used the case to illustrate the nefarious consequences of excessive and unsupervised proselytizations. The sentence meted out to Canon Mallet (six years in prison) reaffirmed the French government's support of the sanctity of the family (Isser, 1979).

Despite the development of communal institutions and self-preserving protests when necessary, these efforts came to naught in Western Europe as the Hitler era and the Holocaust wreaked destruction on Jewish communities. In spite of traumatic and tragic experiences, after the war Jews returned to Holland, France, and even Germany, and attempted to recreate their former sense of identity both as citizens and as Jews. However, the Finaly Affair reawakened the anxieties of the Mortara kidnapping, and exacerbated the fears created by wartime events.

The values, attitudes, and publicity that attended the Finaly case opened emotional wounds and revived bitter and angry memories. To the anti-clericals, the Church reappeared as the old enemy and the threat to liberal ideals (Rémond, 1976, pp.316-317). To the Jews, the old spectre of proselytization appeared even more devastating in the shadow of the Holocaust, and the added anxiety over the fate of the newly-born State of Israel intensified the sense of mutual responsibility and community among French Jews at this time. The combined action of Jewish organizations in the Finaly case led the Church to disavow the earlier ruling of the Mortara case on the baptism of Jewish (and other "non-believing") children. The Anneke Beekman case had a less successful outcome because the Dutch Jewish community was too weak and fragmented to wage a good battle (Fishman, 1978).

Today's communities and proselytization

The problem that we face today is analagous in some ways to these earlier cases. The individual is separated from the family by a religious movement and, as in the past, religious movements of this kind are perceived by the majority of the Jewish community as inimical to its welfare. Two major differences emerge, however, in an examination of the ways in which Jewish children and youth were proselytized in the past and the techniques of proselytization being used today. One is the matter of parental trust. In the Bluth, Finaly, and Beekman cases, children were entrusted to others for education and for protection, and that trust was violated by members of the Church as the children were involuntarily converted. The second difference is the matter of chronological age. In the Mortara, Bluth, Linneweil, Finaly, and Beekman cases, the victims were legally minors. In most of the contemporary cults, the overwhelming majority of converts are legally adults, and hence legally not subject to parental preferences in the matter of religion. Despite these differences, the past and the present are linked by the threads and threats of excessive proselytization and involuntary conversion.

The triumph of secularism and the assimilation of the Jewish community into society at large have accentuated the vulnerability of Jewish adolescents and young adults to proselytization appeals. The rapidity of change in society, already noted, has left young people without a solid base of values and beliefs. Though they claim to seek freedom from parental lifestyles and conformity to social norms, following paths blazed in the rebellious '60's, it is to the highly structured, value-laden, highly conformist groups that they turn for approval, authority, and acceptance.

Unlike the cults, the conservative and reform movements in Judaism are highly intellectual, relatively unemotional, and tend to have minimal structure. Hence, they frequently fail to kindle the loyalty or commitment of their congregants, whose religious practices then lapse. Youths regard their parents' synagogue affiliation, therefore, as hypocritical and superficial. The adolescent is even less committed him/herself, partly because of an inadequate Jewish education, and partly because of the lack of appropriate models in the home. Rejecting institutional values immaturely perceived, the youth turns to a group that offers an opportunity for emotional and experiential involvement.

Response to this evidence of inadequate and ineffective religious education reflects the ambivalence of parents and the adult Jewish community in general. Though vocally supporting both day-school and congregational schools, too often Jewish education is sabotaged when its advocates cite financial costs and personal inconvenience as reasons for not sending their children for instruction beyond Bar/Bat Mitzvah age or for not providing better instructional staffs. The minimal exposure to Jewish values and attitudes in the elementary school years, with little reinforcement of even these at home, rarely leads to their internalization, which would aid the youth in resisting missionary and cult attempts at proselytization. How many young Jews today, confronted with Bible-quoting proselytizers, would have to respond as Alphonse Ratisbonne did that they have no Hebrew text or prayer to offer as a counter-argument and do not know any? Further, the relative ignorance of parents and some Jewish educators regarding the conflict between Jewish values and cult precepts, if not outright antisemitism, contributes as well to the vulnerability of Jewish youth.

Alphonse Ratisbonne, depressed and in poor health (probably psychosomatic in origin), might today have become a member of the Hare Krishna movement or the Unification Church rather than a convert to Catholicism. Similarly, today's cult members might, in that earlier day, have had a visual hallucination that would have led them to active participation in the Church. The mid-nineteenth century, as today, was an era of active missionary activity and frequent episodes of being "born again" into a stronger, more fundamental religious affiliation and commitment. In both periods, the solution to the individual's inner conflicts is withdrawal from the main arena to a more circumscribed and authoritarian area of activity. One explanation of alleged divine intervention in the event is that it is a defense mechanism to ward off the anxiety aroused by a more realistic interpretation of the sudden conversion.

Groups in various sectors of the Jewish community are having more difficulty in combatting these diffuse perils of proselytization today than was true of more specific dangers in former years. Society is more fluid; youths are less constrained by parental injunctions; the cult techniques are swift and emotional, rather than intellectual; and efforts by parents to retrieve their adult children from these groups are being hindered by charges of kidnapping and violation of their children's civil liberties (*Civil Liberties*, September 1977).

The obligations "to make people out of children" and to "train up the child in the way he should go" (Proverbs 22:6) are taken seriously by most Jewish parents. They do not see these obligations ending at age eighteen. Beyond the physical well-being of children, beyond the normal desire to guide children toward free but informed choices as adults, there is a certain anxiety among Jewish parents to maintain the Jewish family in order to ensure the continued existence of the Jewish people. A controversial 1977 Israeli law against missionary efforts that use enticement (money or other concrete inducements) to achieve religious conversions similarly reflects that anxiety. The new battle against the cults and Messianic missions is a further acknowledgement of the dangerous challenge these groups pose to the goal of Jewish survival and continuation.

Common law support of the family as an integral unit of society would appear to give the family the right to resist intrusions on their religious way of life. The family, and by extension the community, is fighting for its child's right to freedom of thought as a prerequisite to freedom of religious choice. Moreover, it is in the interest of the community to maintain this concept of the sanctity of the family by developing legal implementation of the common law principle.

There are those who would dispute this communal obligation. There is some anxiety that, in drawing attention to the problem, others in society will condemn the Jews for not wanting to share religious liberty with other groups. It is ironic that Jewish individuals and organizations, ordinarily highly vocal defenders of civil liberties and religious pluralism, are placed in this position. Their "strident condemnation of cults" (Shupe & Bromley, 1980, p.177) can be understood in terms of an historical emphasis on defending the strong familial values of Judaism. Some researchers, notably several sociologists, characterize today's cult movements as no different from other currently-accepted religious groups that were rejected by society in *their* early stages of development.

Nevertheless, organizations within the Jewish community are beginning to take steps to combat proselytization by the cults and missionary movements. In Philadelphia, the Jewish Community Relations Council (1978) undertook a study of the cult phenomenon and its implications for the community. The Council also co-sponsored, with the local Bar Association, the Catholic Archdiocese, and the Episcopal Diocese, a day-long workshop on the cults which attracted not only parents and professionals concerned with this phenomenon, but also about 75 "Moonies."

The New York counterpart of this group has published a report on "Jews and Jewish Christianity" (Lustiger, 1979), and has created a 24-hour telephone "Cult Hot-Line" to assist individuals and their families who have been affected by cult and missionary activity (Lester, 1980/81). The Union of American Hebrew Congregations has developed a mini-course on "Missionaries and Cult Movements" for use with ninth-graders in religious schools (Daum, 1977). Individual congregations have invited speakers to address their members on the nature of missionary and cult movements. The Jewish press, including both Anglo-Jewish newspapers and professional journals, have increasingly focused their attention on the threatening nature of these groups (Warshaw, 1979, pp.36-40, 103-113).

Concern **is** mounting within the Jewish community about the vulnerability of Jewish youth to proselytization efforts. This is tied to increasing awareness and anxiety that this generation of young Jews may become assimilated and converted more easily and in greater numbers than any previous generation.

On the other hand, there are church groups and cult movements that are actively supporting missionary activity to the Jews and, in some cases, not even perceiving that they are betraying the faith of their founding fathers, Jesus and Paul, who were Jews. The Jewish communities, in their responses to these threats, also exhibit ambivalence. Some perceive the conversion activities as temporary irritants and regard the protesters as paranoid. Some focus on the civil rights issues and aver that children have the right to choose their faith, whether or not the choice may be a mistake with lifelong impact (Lyles, 1977, pp.451-453).

Other members of the Jewish community, seeing any proselytization effort as antisemitic in nature, choose to fight the movement on a more organized community level. They use varied means and media, as we have seen, to combat the pernicious effects of the cults and other evangelical groups. This kind of effort was formalized during the Mortara Affair and is the means by which Jews have responded in more recent years to the needs of their co-religionists in Rumania, Russia, France, Germany, and Israel. The founding of the Alliance Israelite Universelle in 1861 was the forerunner of a continuing international cooperation which has become traditional when threats to Jewish welfare appear anywhere in the world. As a result of such cooperation, Jewish communities have developed cohesive and effective methods of coping with some crises in the Diaspora.

The threat to the present and future generations of Judaism is thought to be great enough that united action in preventive and remedial measures is warranted. That effort must respond not only to the cults, however, but also to the total threat to the continuity of Jewish life.

> If we are to prevent kids from joining cults, we must provide them with the best antidote we have to prevent assimilation and intermarriage: warm, lively, interesting Jewish communities with religious values, communities that care about people (*Israel*, 1979, p.1346).

The alienation, the narcissism, and the general breakdown of family life that characterized the late 1970's, leaving a vacuum for young people at a most critical point in their psychosocial development, must be turned around if the Jewish community is to survive for many more generations. In summarizing several studies of psychological deviance among Jews, Sanua concluded that "family solidarity and identification with one's group tend to reduce the incidence of alcoholism, drug addiction, suicide," and, it might be added, affiliation with other religions or cults (Sanua, 1974, pp.297-312).

Although many cults have adopted a lower profile in the wake of the mass suicide in Guyana of People's Temple cult members, the belief that the threat they pose will disappear, is considered erroneous. Even if it did, the fundamental problems of proselytization will continue. Other, more orthodox groups such as the Mormons, Seventh Day Adventists, Jehovah's Witnesses, and diverse evangelical sects will continue to attempt to attract Jewish youth, and even adults — especially as the milennium draws closer. The challenge to the Jewish community will remain: to adopt a more vital relgious lifestyle and cultural environment that will involve creative, constructive participation and commitment on the part of the Jewish young people. They seek an opportunity for meaningful commitment to a "good cause" and it must be supplied. McGowan (1979) pointed out that, in this respect, traditional religions can take lessons from the cults. Youths want to see the brotherhood and the fine principles expressed on the Sabbath in practice during the rest of the week. No rabbi or other clergy-person could quarrel with that goal, and each would be only too pleased to welcome and witness it in his/her congregation.

Despite the fact that cult members appear to welcome the ritual practices of their respective groups, most adolescents and young adults reject traditional religious ritual as meaningless. Unless they are shown the psychological value inherent in ritual and observance, and taught to be comfortable with them, people — and this would be more likely true for converts to Christianity — are likely to reject not only such practices, but all things Jewish (Diller, 1980, p.42). Therefore, if Jews believe that there is a rationale for a ritual, they must find ways to convey that rationale more effectively. Spero (1977), for example, has suggested stressing the vitality of past and current Jewish teachings and perspective. In general, through acceptance of the fact of Jewish identity, awareness of personal feelings toward that identity exposure to a more satisfying perspective on Jewish heritage,. such as suggested by Spero, the individual must be led to a meaningful means of Jewish self-expression which can play a central role in one's life activity (Diller, 1980, p.43).

Half a century ago, Louis Marshall, then head of the American Jewish Committee, wrote that

> When Jews rebel against interference with their most sacred right, that of religious liberty, when Jewish parents seek to protect their children for whose moral and ethical life they feel a serious responsibility, against the intrusion and trespasses of conversionists, it is the Jews who are interfering with religious liberty, because, forsooth! they are undertaking to muzzle Christians and are interfering with free speech (in Sklare, 1973, p.48).

Nevertheless, whether the community today chooses to maintain its own life profile, as some would do, or takes an aggressive stance, perhaps only slightly less militant than that of the Jewish Defense League, it must assert its opposition to proselytization. If Catholics want to appeal to lapsed members of their faith, or Protestants to recalcitrant ex-parishioners, or Chassidim to less observant Jews — all of them seeking to bring lost sheep back into the fold — no one can be hostile toward that effort. However, other groups have been threatened and assailed by the conversion efforts of the cults and have responded to those efforts in different fashion.

Just as Jews as a community have reacted negatively to proselytization, established Christian groups have reacted with suspicion and distress to the implication of the cults, for the community, the guardian for the care and the transmission of culture, is responsible for its own perpetuation and survival. Hence, deviant and nonconformist religions pose a challenge to the **group** as well as the family, especially if it is a proselytizing cult. That factor is self evident as history too sadly illustrates. The group generally distrusts "the other," but, if threatened, that dislike can be transformed into passionate fury and result in conflict or persecution, or perhaps, harassment, depending upon the nature of the society and its attitude toward human rights.

In those cases, however, where deviant religious groups present a position that is more than being "the other" or different, that is, their religious doctrines are contrary to the norms and the values of the community, the opposition can be measured in legal restraints rather than persecution alone. Thus one of the reasons for the anger against the Mormons was their practice of polygamy, a ritual forbidden by the State. Other cults such as Father Divine's or the Shakers have been tolerated so long as they did not proselytize too actively or their doctrines reflected the communities' values. As the deviant sects such as the Mormons or Christian Scientists either muted or rejected doctrines perceived as inimical to the larger society, they were accepted as part of the mainstream religions.

Presently, the community (in the United States, Europe, Israel, and elsewhere) has been confronted once more with the proliferation of numerous religious or quasi-religious movements. Some have been perceived as dangerous, deviant, non-conformist and socially undesirable because of their suspicious recruiting methods. Furthermore, many of the cults urge the isolation of their members and channel the energies of their committed believers into fund raising activities of questionable value. Many in the community, as well as parents directly concerned, became alarmed at what they sensed is not only the disruption of young adult lives, but also the loss of exceptional talents important to the future of the group and society (Conway & Siegelman, 1978). This has led to the formation of anti-cult groups, and to agitation to limit some of the cults' more questionable activities.

Unfortunately, some parents, distraught by the loss of their adult children, have resorted to methods which are just as ruthless and destructive as those attributed to some cults. Psychologically, we raise our children to become self-sufficient adults, able to live independently away from home. However, when these young adults make decisions that are disruptive to the family, some parents have responded by assuming that their grown children are **not** adults and then have resorted to kidnapping and deprogramming. That such methods are both immoral and illegal is not open to question. Obviously "brainwashing" even in a good cause is reprehensible, and deprogramming **is** thought control in reverse. Furthermore, it has been these activities, more than anything else, that has brought the anti-cult movement into disrepute in some quarters and caused protests by some sociologists (Shupe & Bromley, 1980) and other liberals against the zealous opposition to such groups.

Others, most prominently the American Civil Liberties Union (ACLU), devoted to the principle of religious freedom, vehemently defend the "rights" of minority religions. They are supported by a few within the Jewish community, such as Rabbi Polish and constitutional lawyer Jeremiah Gutman, who, fearful of any attack on any minority groups, attract anti-cult activity (Melton & Moore, 1982).

Some researchers and scholars have characterized today's cult movements as being no different from other currently-accepted religious groups that were rejected by society in their early stages of development. They make sweeping accusations against those who are opposed to these cults that range from naiveté to anti-civil-libertarianism, from ignorance to greed. They ignore the privations, duplicity, and manipulative techniques that they themselves have witnessed, justifying all with the blessings of adulthood and the protection of the First Amendment. They omit any consideration, except in the most negative sense, of the parent-child relationship and of the ripple effect of cult membership (or conversion) on family members. Terming some of the cults "world-transforming groups" (Shupe & Bromley, 1980, pp.233-237), they appear to condone the destruction of an admittedly imperfect society rather than seeking constructive remedies for its deficiencies.

The contrary arguments by mental health professionals do not fully detail the reasons why so many of them (some of whom are neither in clinical practice nor parents of in-cult or ex-cult members) are opposed to the practices of today's cults. They are disturbed by the deception they perceive in recruiting that leads to decision making on the basis of limited, and sometimes false, information. If members of the

Mormon Church or Jehovah's Witnesses, often linked in
terms of **their** early history and continuing proselytizing
efforts, approach someone, they introduce themselves **and**
their religious affiliation before "witnessing." If the prospect
continues to listen or chooses to follow them, it is with
"informed consent" and not on the basis of half-truths,
evasions, or other deceptions.

In some of the new religions, mental health professionals
perceive physiological and psychological manipulation that
is designed to make recruits highly susceptible to whatever
suggestions are made by group members. They see also
exploitation of the unwary, abuse of trust, and destruction of
family relationships, all of which they deplore. In some
instances, they have also observed child abuse and sought to
have children's custody changed in the children's best
interests. One has only to recall the tragedy of Jonestown to
perceive the problems created in and by some cults.

On the other hand, there are over 2000 cult groups in the
United States alone. A very large number do not use these
tactics or behave with excessive missionary zeal or resort to
questionable fund-raising methods. They may advocate an
alternative life-style and may be eccentric in their vision of
the universe, but their activities are legitimate. The issues we
have raised could be applied to *any* group, however,
mainstream or minority, that employs overzealousness or
questionable methods of indoctrination.

One does not have to be labeled intolerant or prejudiced
to object to initial (or later) deception by religious or other
groups (Langone, 1986). Indeed, deception is inconsistent
with the morality presumably espoused by religious groups.

The elements shared by religious and evangelical missionaries in the nineteenth century, "thought reform" as practiced in wartime Korea in the 1950's, and techniques used by some of today's cults are equally unacceptable (Schwartz & Isser, 1981). In each case, manipulation of emotions such as fear, guilt, and love, usually in the absence of competing information, is used as the primary means to proselytize and convert the individual. The fact that this manipulation has been used successfully by political and religious groups for centuries does not justify its continued use.

EPILOGUE

On 3 April 1977, it was reported in *The New York Times* that the sixth meeting of the International Catholic-Jewish liaison committee had issued a declaration denouncing proselytization of Jews. The article further stated that "the legacy of forced conversion of Jews has posed formidable problems for ecumenical talks even as the climate between the two faiths has warmed since the Second Vatican Council" (*The New York Times*, 3 April 1977). Although the Second Vatican Council had condemned anti-semitism, it had not rejected proselytizing practices. In response to the new declaration, Rabbi Henry Siegman, a conference participant, said: "The memory of forced conversions is deeply ingrained in the consciousness of the Jewish people and has been the most serious obstacle to the development of Christian-Jewish relations" (ibid.).

Isaac Rottenberg, son of a convert to Christianity and grandson of a rabbi, supported this view as he pointed out that most Christian clergy are unaware of such actions despite having studied church history. In a review of the cruelties perpetrated by Christians against the people they called "Christ-killers," Rottenberg asked, "Is it surprising then that to so many Jews conversion came to mean 'joining the enemy'?" (Rottenberg, 1977, pp.353-354)

Another interfaith conference, this one between evangelical Christians and Jews, took place in December 1980. Goals of the conference were to reaffirm tolerance for religious pluralism and to denounce anti-semitism. Fears expressed by some of the Jewish conferees included the view that proselytization of Jewish youth would lead to cultural genocide. "At the same time, the evangelical Christians maintained that noncoercive, non-deceptive means of evangelism were not necessarily anti-semitic and they vowed to continue the efforts as a mandate of their faith" (Briggs, 1980). One evangelical scholar, certainly far less sensitive than Rottenberg, "advocated doing away with the term 'conversion.' He called it a red herring for Jews and an unbiblical way of describing the mysterious change of heart that comes with religious knowledge" (Buursma, 1981). He could not comprehend, apparently, that, more than the term, the practice is what disturbs Jews. Part of the uproar stems from the increasing campaigns by "Hebrew Christian" groups, as well as others, to convert Jewish youth.

In contrast to the voiced rejection of proselytization by some Catholic leaders, the Jewish community is confronted by the militant proselytizing efforts of evangelical, Messianic, and cult groups on college campuses and elsewhere. These campaigns pose a threat to a Jewish community already endangered by less exotic but potentially more lethal plagues of intermarriage, assimilation, and ignorance (Israel, 1980). The absolute numbers of young people enmeshed in all of these groups may be relatively small, but the community can ill afford to lose any of the new adult generation of Jews.

The significance of forced conversions and excessive proselytization, as shown in the preceding chapters, resides ultimately in the importance Jews place upon family life. The family in the Jewish tradition is as important as it is in

Christianity, perhaps even more so since the home has been a center for worship and observance of religious festivals, serving as primary a function as that of the synagogue. Thus, threats to the family structure and its welfare — that is conversion, assimilation, intermarriage — strike at the very heart of Jewish life, its beliefs, its social structure, its very survival. Proselytization, in short, has been and is still perceived as a continuing and durable enemy.

Medieval Jewry, Sephardic Jewry, and even most contemporary Jews, have expressed concern not only about conversions **of** Jews but conversions **to** Judaism. This concern has been derived from the defensive, sometimes precarious, position of Jewish communities in the Diaspora over the centuries. Rabbi Simon Luria in the mid-sixteenth century felt that proselytizing by Jews would endanger their survival (Rosenbloom, 1978). Seventeenth-century English Jews, newly restored to England after 350 years of banishment, not only enacted anti-proselytizing laws, but in 1671 forbade even the temporary employment of Christian maids, an interesting antecedent of the 19th century Papal law involved in the Mortara case (Rosenbloom, 1978). It is apparent from these brief references that the Jewish community responded to conversion — both apostasy and proselytization — negatively. On the one hand, they felt the diminution of the community by every individual who converted to Christianity, and on the other, they felt imperiled by every individual who sought to convert to Judaism. Generally, however, their responses to these threats were unique to specific communities rather than national or international. Multi-community action really began, as we noted in Chapter VI, in the nineteenth century.

As John Donne stated so eloquently, "No man is an island entire of itself...," so every individual's actions have a ripple effect on others, especially upon his family and community. Conversion and commitment, as we have illustrated, thus command emotional consequences for families and often engage the community's concern. Such activity has been an ongoing historical phenomenon in Western societies for centuries. Currently, however, the plethora of new cults and sects have once more focused attention upon this long-standing problem.

Despite all parental and community opposition, despite the lower profile of some suspect contemporary groups, conversion as a phenomenon will continue, whether the proselytization is active or muted. For the individual who is seeking solace or new resources to solve ever-recurring problems in a world she cannot control, she will convert for the variety of reasons already cited (Chapter 1). Such conversions may indeed assist the troubled individual to cope, and/or may cause enormous distress to family and community members. Whether the alteration is from one established religion to another, or to an esoteric cult or secular organization, such personal choices represent the individual's response to his/her emotional needs. How successful the choice is depends on individual circumstances.

Often, the rebellion against the establishment or against what the young considered the soulless, corrupt, and alienated technological society led, as we have already observed, not to deviant or even peculiar religious groups, but rather to a renewal or a resurgence of faith in non-conventional movements (at least among those in the mobile upper-middle-class society). The popularity of "Born again"

Christianity or the Christian Crusade on College Campuses, or secular quasi-therapy movements such as *est* or "Life-Spring" are a reflection of such quests.

Young Jews who were not able to reject their roots or tradition so totally expressed their indignation at modern life by turning instead to Orthodoxy, especially in the late 1960's and 1970's, but continuing well into the 1980's. This acceptance of an older tradition reflected revulsion to on-going cultural ideals, but their hostility to the establishment was channeled back into **traditional** values in a search for a more purified and idealized past. Because in many cases this behavior involves a dismantling of secularization, this re-channeling often occurs in the same fashion as with those who have returned to fundamental Christianity, and, because it involves adopting new values and life-styles, it can be equivalent to conversion as in other religions (Aviad, 1980).

On the other hand, those individuals who have opted for membership in a variety of cults rebel in a far more disturbing manner. As already discussed in Chapter III, many of these cults alienate the larger society because they are so organized as to be separated from the community. They have adopted new and strange ideologies accompanied by equally variant life-styles. These configurations, in the eyes of some in the community, deny their legitimacy. Furthermore, some cults and sects feel that they have, exclusively, the "Truth" and are, therefore, superior to the rest of humanity. Their aberrant rules and behavior are the outgrowth of their sense of elitism, enabling them (in their own eyes) to ignore rules that regulate the rest of the community. Inevitably, antagonism and confrontation erode the relationship between cults and the rest of society (Appel, 1983).

Undoubtedly, affective bonds are forged during the commitment to the alternative group, and those connections often become an important, even a critical, part of conversion. Studies have indicated that many who do convert seem to have fewer meaningful relationships prior to their change (Greil & Rudy, 1981). Thus the social bonding that sometimes becomes the focus of the individual's attention and the source of affective relationships poses an even more effective break between the individual and his/her family. Both the family and the social group have suffered an irreparable loss, a loss which either or both may challenge with hostility and/or anguish.

The individual who chooses freely to convert, thus abandoning his past, causes unwitting dismay to his family and community. However, those who do advocate salvation by active proselytization (be it from mainstream faiths or the off-beat sects) need to be and should be more sensitive to the emotional ramifications of their behavior. As we have observed in the historical data, missionary activity, whether from the mainstream faiths or others, if overzealously pursued, can have unpredictable consequences, wrecking families and exacerbating group hostilities .

Jews are the most sensitive to the threat of proselytization because they are the most targeted group for missionaries, although other communities have, in the past as now, felt the same animosities. Catholics in nineteenth-century France bitterly attacked the Protestant minority, largely because of their ardent evangelical activities. In many developing countries today, as in India and Israel, laws have been passed restricting the activities of missionaries. The very act of missionary preaching implies that "theirs" is a superior message, that the group outside their faith is denied salvation, or "the light" and "truth." In short, no matter how the message is delivered, with or without tact, the underlying theme is a subtle denigration of the other's beliefs and values. Hence, antagonism or latent hostility can result among those solicited. This fact is even more apparent as we indicated earlier, in the manipulative and occasionally unscrupulous tactics used by some cults. But other groups, most notably "Jews for Jesus"-type groups, exhibit equally great insensitivity in their search for converts.

It is our conviction and conclusion, as a result of examining the events and effects of conversion in the cases presented here, that active, zealous proselytization, seeking to separate an individual from his/her faith for the purpose of converting that individual to another faith, is morally wrong. Attempts to restore faith in lapsed former members is not questioned. Our objection is to the organized, emotional, and excessive persuasion exercised by the members of one faith to create new followers from another faith that frequently has tenets that are contradictory, and sometimes inimical, to that of the original religion. The psychological havoc created for the individual, the wrenching apart of families, and the hostility generated between religious communities all testify to the negative consequences of such proselytizing behaviors.

In the United States, where freedom of religious choice is a constitutional right and where pluralism is espoused, there is a legitimate freedom to change religions if one so desires.

The assumption underlying that statement is that such a conversion is rationally based and that the individual perceives and anticipates the conflicts that may arise. (This does not imply, however, the presence of psychopathology in the absence of such perception.) There is an implication of informed choice in the decision. Badgering, "siege" techniques, emotional appeals in unusual settings, and "heavenly deception" do not lead to an informed choice. Isolation from those who might protest the sudden conversion or those who might recognize the psychological problems that may underlie it does not lead to an informed or rational choice. Yet these are all tools of manipulative people who would lead an individual to make a major change in his commitments for their benefit — a step on the road to salvation or a sense of inner satisfaction, for example — rather than his own, and would have him do it quickly before he can consider the ramifications of his decision. To us, this practice contradicts and violates precepts held and preached by churches and synagogues. It is, therefore, a threat to these very faiths and a moral error. Furthermore, to the Jewish community, proselytization is a threat to the survival of a people, and conversion is correctly perceived as an anathema.

Just as Jews as a community have reacted negatively to proselytization, established Christian groups have reacted with suspicion and distress to the intrusion of the cults. However, Christians of all denominations have as a basic tenet themselves a commitment to evangelizing their faith. In the face of the consequences of the Holocaust and their own conflicts with varying cults, some leaders have eschewed missionary efforts, especially toward the Jews (Eckardt, 1967). Twenty years later, "Disputing for the first time the evangelistic dictum that Jews are religiously doomed without Jesus, conventions of two major Protestant denominations have recently said that Jews have a continuing covenant with God that should be respected" (Dart, 1987). The two groups are the United Church of Christ and the Presbyterian Church (U.S.A.). As Dart continued, "Liberal Protestant churches rarely endorse or engage in evangelism among Jewish people, but neither have they been eager to disavow entirely the traditional concept of proclaiming their beliefs to anyone who will listen" (Dart, 1987). They have not abandoned the precept to spread the Gospel, but have chosen to convey their beliefs by example. If all religious groups chose such methods of proselytization, the level of conflict and resentment would be decreased; the principles of tolerance, of regarding all religious beliefs as legitimate, and of respect for varying points of view would be observed in practice; and the observance of religious pluralism in the United States would be served.

REFERENCES

Adler, W. (1978, June 6). Rescuing David from the Moonies. *Esquire*, **3** (10), pp. 23-30.

Allison, J. (1968). Adaptive regression and intense religious experiences. *Journal of Nervous and Mental Disease*, **145**, 452-463.

Allison, J. (1969) Religious conversion: regression and progression in an adolescent experience. *Journal for the Scientific Study of Religion*, **8** (1), 23-38.

American Psychiatric Association. (1980). *Diagnostic and statistical manual of mental disorders* (3rd ed.). Washington, D.C.: Author.

Appel, J.J. (1969). Religious conversion: regression and progression in an adolescent experience. *Journal for the Scientific Study of Religion*, **31** (2), 100-121.

Appel, W. (1983). *Cults in America: Programmed for paradise.* New York: Holt, Rinehart, & Winston.

Archives Departmentales, MSS. Haut-Loire, Puy de Dôme.

Archives Israélites. (1860, 1861, 1864) newspaper.

Archives Nationales, Paris, MSS. F19, Ministry of Religion, cartons 1789, 1937.

Arendt, H. (1974). *Rahel Varnhagen, The life of a Jewish woman.* (R. & C. Winston, Trans.). Revised edition. New York: Harcourt, Brace, Jovanovich.

Aviad, J. (1980, Summer). From protest to return: Contemporary teshuvah. *The Jerusalem Quarterly*, **16**, pp.71-82.

Balch, R.W. (1980). Looking behind the scenes in a religious cult: Implications for the study of conversion. *Sociological Analysis*, **41** 23., 137-143.

Baron, S.W. (1976). Changing patterns of anti-semitism: A survey. *Jewish Social Studies*, **5**, 5-38.

Baudy, N. (1953). The affair of the Finaly children. *Commentary*, **15**, 547-557.

Beckford, J.A. (1976). Organization, ideology, and recruitment: the structure of the Watch Tower Movement. *Sociological Review*, **23** 893-909.

Beckford, J.A. (1978a). Accounting for conversion. *British Journal of Sociology*, **29** (2), 249-262.

Beckford, J.A. (1978b). Cults and cures. *Japanese Journal of Religious Studies*, **5**, 225-254.

Beckford, J.A. (1978c). Through the looking-glass and out the other side: Withdrawal from Reverend Moon's Unification Church. *Archives de Sciences Sociales des Religions*, **45** (1), 95-116.

Beckford, J.A. (1979). Politics and the anti-cult movement. *Annual Review of the Social Sciences of Religion*, **3**.

Belford, Lee A. (1977). Sun Myung Moon and the Unification Church. *Intellect*, **105**, 336-337.

Berger, P.L., Berger, B. & Kellner, H. (1973). *The homeless mind*. New York: Random House.

Bernstein, M. (1979). *The nuns.* New York: Bantam Books.

Blanchard, P. (1960). *Le vénérable Libermann: 1802-1852.* 2 Vol. Paris: Desclée de Brouver.

Bowlby, J. (1958). The nature of the child's tie to his mother. *International Journal of Psychoanalysis,* **39,** 350-373.

Bowlby, J. (1961). Processes of meaning. *International Journal of Psychoanalysis,* **42** (4-5), 317-340.

Briggs, K.A. (1980, December 14). Leaders of Jews and evangelical Christians work for better relations between faiths. *The New York Times.,* p. L32.

Bromley, D.G. (1985). Cults: facts and fictions. *VCU Magazine,* **14** (2), 10-15.

Brown, M. (1977). *Louis Veuillot.* Durham, N.C.: Moore Publishing Co.

Buursma, B. (1981, January 4). Jews wary of "decade of danger." *Philadelphia Inquirer.*

Cantril, H. & Sherif, M. (1938). The kingdom of Father Divine. *Journal of Abnormal Psychology,* **33,** 147-167.

Carmelle, Sister M. (Ed.). (1977). *Sources de Sion.* 2 Volumes. Paris. Privat.

Chalfont, H. Paul, Buckley, R.E. & Palmer, C.E. (1981). *Religion in contemporary society.* Sherman Oaks, CA: Alfred Publishing.

Charity Frauds Bureau. (1974, September 30). Final Report on the Children of God to Hon. Louis J. Lefkowitz, Attorney General of the State New York (mimeo).

Christensen, C.W. (1963). Religious conversion. *Archives of General Psychiatry*, **9**, 207-216.

Civil LIberties. (1977, September).

Clark, J.G., Jr. (1979). Cults. *Journal of the American Medical Association*, **242**, 274-281.

Clark, K. (1963). *Prejudice and your child*, 2nd Ed. Boston: Beacon Press.

Coe, G.A. (1900). *The spiritual life*. New York: Eaton & Mains.

Conway, F. & Siegelman, J. (1978). *Snapping*. Philadelphia : Lippincott.

Cox, H. (1977). Why young Americans are buying Oriental religions. *Psychology Today*, **11** (2), 36-42.

Cox, L. (1986). Hope for a shattered heart. *Virtue*, 8 (7), 40-42.

Cunningham, A., Nelson, J.R., Hendricks, W.L., & Lara-Brand, J. (1978). Critique of the theology of the Unification Church as set forth in *Divine Principle* .In I. L. Horowitz (ed.), *Science, sin and scholarhip: The politics of reverend Moon and the Unification Church* (pp. 102-118). Cambridge, MA: The M.I.T. Press.

Damrell, J. (1978). *Search for identity: Youth, religion and culture*. Beverly Hills, CA.: Sage.

Daner, F.J.. (1976). *The American children of KRSNA : A study of the HARE KRSNA movement*. New York: Holt, Rinehart and Winston.

Dansette, A. (1961). *Religious history of modern France*, 2 vols. (trans., J.Dingle). New York: Herder and Herder.

Dart, J. (1987, July 13). Two Protestant groups affirm a formal respect for Judaism. *The Philadelphia Inquirer*, p.2-A.

Daum, A. (1977). Missionary and cult movements, a mini-course in the Upper Grades in religious schools. New York: Union of American Hebrew Congregations.

Deutsch, A. (1975). Observations on a sidewalk ashram. *Archives of General Psychiatry*, **32**, 166-175.

Diller, J.V. (1980). Identity, rejection and reawakening in the Jewish context. *Journal of Psychology and Judaism*, **5** (1), 38-47.

Downton, J.J., Jr. (1979). *Sacred journeys: The conversion of young Americans to Divine Light Mission*. New York: Coumbia University Press.

Downton, J.J., Jr. (1980). An evolutionary theory of spiritual conversion and commitment: The case of Divine Light Mission. *Journal for the Scientific Study of Religion*, **19**, 381-396.

Drach, D.P. (1825) . *Lettre d'un rabbi converti aux Israélites ses frères sur les motifs de sa conversion*. Paris.

Drach, D.P. (1827). *Deuxième lettre d'un rabbi converti aux Israélites a ses frères sur les motifs de sa conversion*. Paris.

Drach, D.P. (1828). *Rélation de la conversion de M. Hyacinthe Deutz, baptisé a Rome le 3 fevrier 1828*. Brussels.

Drach, D.P.(1833). *Troisième lettre d'un rabbi converti aux Israélites a ses frères sur les motifs de sa conversion*. Paris.

Ebaugh, H.R.F. (1977). *Out of the cloister*. Austin: University of Texas. Press.

Eckardt, R.A. (1967). *Elder and younger brothers: The encounter of Jews and Christians*. New York: Shocken.

Edwards, C. (1979). *Crazy for God*. Englewood Cliffs, N. J.: Prentice-Hall.

Eichorn, D.M. (1965). *Conversion to Judaism, A history and analysis*. New York : Ktav.

Enroth, R.M., Ericson, E.S., Jr., &Peters, B. C. (1972). *The Jesus People: Old time religion in the Age of Aquarius*. Grand Rapids, MI: Erdmann.

Entin, A.D. (1982). Family icons: Photographs in family psychotherapy. In L. Abt & I. Stuart (Eds.), *The newer therapies: A sourcebook* (pp.206-227). New York: Van Nostrand.

Ericson, E.E., Jr., & McPherson, P. (1973, July 20). The deceptions of the Children of God. *Christianity Today*, pp. 14-20.

Erikson, E.H. (1950). *Childhood and Society*. New York: W.W. Norton.

Erikson, E.H. (1956).The problem of ego identity. *American Psychoanalytic Association Journal*, **4**, 56-121.

Evans, E.N. (1973). *The provincials*. New York: Atheneum.

Ferm, R. O. (1959). *The psychology of Christian conversion*. Westward, N. J.: Fleming H. Revell Co.

Fishman, J.S. (1978) Anneke Beekman Affair and the Dutch news media. *Jewish Social Studies*, **40**, 3-24.

Flannery, E.H. (1965). *The Anguish of the Jews*. New York, London: McMillan.

Fogarty, R.S. (1981). *The Righteous Remnant, the House of David*. Ohio: Kent State University Press.

France-Soir. (1978, July 25). The Finaly case twenty-five years later.

Freedman, J.L. & Fraser, S.C. (1966). Compliance without pressure: the "foot-in-the-door" technique. *Journal of Personality and Social Psychology*, **4**, 195-202.

Freud, A. & Burlingham, D. (1943). *War and children*. New York: Medical War Books.

Freud, S. (1922/1959). *Group psychology and the analysis of the ego* (J.Strachey, Ed. & Trans.). New York: W.W. Norton.

Friedlander, S. (1979a, April). An extraordinary Catholic childhood. *Commentary*, **67**, pp. 157-166.

Friedlander, S. (1979b). *When Memory Comes*. New York: Giroux.

Fromm, E. (1939). Selfishness and self-love. *Psychiatry*, **2**, 507-523.

Fromm, E. (1950). *Psychoanalysis and religion*. New Haven, Conn : Yale University Press.

Galanter, M. (1983). Unification Church ("Moonie") drop-outs: Psychological readjustment after membership in a charismatic religious group. *American Journal of Psychiatry*, **140**, 984 -989.

Galanter, M. (1986). "Moonies" get married: A psychiatric follow-up study of a charismatic religious sect. *American Journal of Psychiatry*, **143**, 1245-1249.

Galanter, M., & Buckley, P. (1978). Evangelical religion and meditation: Psychotherapeutic effects. *Journal of Nervous and Mental Disease*, **166**, 685-691.

Gazette d'Utrecht (1859, August 12). Newspaper.

Gidney, W.T. (1908). *The history of the London Society for promoting Christianity amongst the Jews, from 1809 to 1908.* London.

Gillespie, V.B. (1979). *Religious conversion and personal identity: How and why people change.* Birmingham, Alabama: Religious Education Press.

Gillis, J.W. (1976, August). Rev. Sun Myung Moon: "Heavenly deception," *Trial,* 22-25.

Gittelsohn, R.B. (1979). Jews for Jesus — Are they real? *Midstream,* **25** (5), pp. 41-45.

Glanz, D. & Harrison, M.L. (1978). Varieties of identity transformation. The case of newly Orthodox Jews. *Jewish Journal of Sociology,* **20**, pp. 129-142.

Gordon, A. (1967). *The Nature of conversion.* Boston: Beacon.

Graeber, I. & Britt, S., (Eds.) .(1942). *Jews in a gentile world, the problem of antisemitism.* New York: Macmillan.

Greil, A. & Rudy, D.R. (1981). What do we know about the conversion process? Paper presented at the Annual Meeting of the Society for the Scientific Study of Religion, Baltimore.

Guitton, J. (1964). *La conversion de Ratisbonne*. Paris: Wesmaelo-Charlier.

Hankoff, L.D. (1979). Adolescence and the crisis of dying. In L.D. Hankoff (Ed.) & B. Einsidler (Assoc.Ed.), *Suicide: Theory and clinical aspects* (pp.201-214). Littleton, MA: PSG Publishing Company.

Hansen, K. (1982). Newsletter of ex-members of the Children of God. mimeo.

Hall, G.S. (1904). *Adolescence*. 2 Vol. New York, Appleton.

Hallie, P. (1980). *Lest innocent blood be shed*. New York: Harper & Row.

Harrigan, J E. (1979). Brainwashing in small groups, China or America: A counselor's view. *Personnel and Guidance Journal*, **148** (1), 16-19.

Harris, S. (1954). *The incredible Father Divine*. London: W. W. Allen.

Harrison, J.F.C. *The Second Coming. Millenarianism 1780-1781*, New Brunswick, N. J.: Rutgers University Press.

Heirich, M. (1977). Change of heart: A test of some widely held theories about religious conversion. *American Journal of Sociology* **83**, 853-680.

Hentig, H.V. (1948). *The criminal and his victim: Studies in the sociology of crime*. New Haven: Yale University Press.

Herbut, P. (1980, December 7). Moonies seek way to improve a "bad" image. *The Evening Bulletin* (Philadelphia).

214

Herman, S. (1977). *Jewish identity : A social psychological perspective*. Beverly Hill, CA., London: Sage.

Holt, R.R. (1964). Forcible indoctrination and personality change. In P.Worchel & Byrne, D. (Eds.) *Personality change*. (pp. 289-318). New York: John Wiley.

Hopkins, J.M . (1969, Nov. 21) . Scientology: Religion or racket? *Christianity Today*, **14**, 10-13.

Hyman, P. (1979). *From Dreyfus to Vichy, the remaking of French Jewry 1906-1939*. New York: Columbia University Press.

Israel, R.J. (1979, Oct. 5). The Kosherei Revolution. *Christianity Today*, **165**.

Israel, R.J. (1980, January). The cult problem is a fake! *The National Jewish Monthly*, pp. 34-37.

Isser, N. (1979, Fall). The Mallet Affair: a case study of scandal. *Revue des Études Juives*, **138**, 291-305.

Isser, N. (1981). The Mortara Affair and Louis Veuillot. *Proceedings of the Western Society for French History*, **7**, pp. 69-78.

Isser, N. (1984) The Linneweil Affair: A study in adolescent vulnerability. *Adolescence*, **19**, pp. 529-643.

Isser, N., & Schwartz, L.L. (1980a). Community responses to the proselytization of Jews. *Journal of Jewish Communal Service*, **57** (1), 663-672.

Isser, N., & Schwartz, L.L. (1980b). Charismatic leadership: A case in point. Paper presented at the Annual meeting of the International Psychohistorical Association, New York.

Isser, N., & Schwartz, L.L. (1980c). Sudden conversion: A psychohistorical view. Paper presented at the Annual meeting of the Association for Jewish Studies, Boston.

Isser, N., & Schwartz, L.L. (1983a). Sudden conversion: The case of Alphonse Ratisbonne. *Jewish Social Studies,* **45** (1),17-30.

Isser, N., & Schwartz, L.L. (1983b). Minority self hate, a psychohistorical case study. *Journal of Psychology and Judaism,* **7** (2), 101-117.

Isser, N., & Schwartz, L.L. (1986). Charismatic leadership: a case in point. *Cultic Studies Journal,* **3** (1), 57-77.

James, W. (1902/1958). *Varieties of religious experience.* New York Mentor Books.

Jewish Community Relations Council of Philadelphia (1978). *The challenge of the cults.* Mimeo.

Journal de Bruxelles. (1860). Newspaper.

Juster, D.C. (1977). Jewishness and Jesus. Downers Grove, Ill.: Intervarsity Press. (pamphlet).

Kanter, R.M. (1972). *Commitment and community: Communes and Utopias in sociological perspective.* Cambridge, Mass: Harvard University Press.

Kaslow, F.W., & Schwartz, L.L. (1983). Vulnerability and invulnerability to cults: An assessment of family dynamics, functioning and values. In D. Bagorozzi, A. Jurich, & R.W. Jackson(Eds.), *Marital and family therapy: New perspectives in theory, research, and practice* (pp.165-190). New York : Human Sciences Press.

Keller, M. (1960). *L'affaire Finaly.* Paris : Fischbacher.

Kemeny, J. (1979). Comment: On Foss, Daniel A. and Ralph W. Larkin, Worshipping the absurd: The negation of social causality among the followers of Guru Maharaj Ji. *Sociological Analysis*, **39** (12), *Sociological Analysis*, **40**, 262-264.

Kemperman, S. (1981). *Lord of the Second Advent: A rare look inside the terrifying world of the Moonies*. Ventura, CA. : Regal Books.

Keniston, K. (1960, 1965). *The uncommitted: Alienated youth in American society*. New York : Harcourt, Brace & World.

Kephart, W.M. (1982). *Extraordinary groups: The sociology of unconventional life-styles*, 2nd ed. New York : St. Martin's Press.

Kilbourne, B.K., & Richardson, J.T. (1986). The communalization of religious experience in contemporary religious groups. *Journal of Community Psychology*, **14**, 206-212.

Kildahl, J.P. (1965). The personalities of sudden religious converts. *Pastoral Psychology*, **16** (156), pp. 37-45.

Klein, P. (1951). Mauvais juif, mauvais chrétien. *Revue de la Pensée Juive*, **7**, 87-103.

Korn, B. (1958). *The American reaction to the Mortara Affair*. Cincinnati: American Jewish Archives. Kselman, T. A. (1983). *Miracles and prophecies in nineteenth century France*. New Brunswick: Rutgers University Press.

Kuehnelt-Leddihn, E.M. Von. (1946, Dec.) . Do Jews make good Catholics? *(New) Catholic World*, **164**, 212-216.

Langone, M.D. (1986). Cults, evangelicals, and the ethics of social influence. *Cultic Studies Journal*, **2**, 371-388.

Lazerwitz, B. (1971). Intermarriage and conversion: A guide for future research. *Jewish Journal of Sociology*, **13 (1)**, 41-63.

Le Monde (1858-1864). Newspaper

Lester, E. (1980-81, Dec. 28- Jan. 4). Cultists focussing on young Jews as prime prospects. *The Jewish Week-American Examiner*. Flushing, N.Y.

Levin, T.N., & Zegans, L.S. (1947). Adolescent identity crisis and religious conversion. *British Journal of Medical Psychology*, 73-82.

Levine, E.M. (1980a). Deprogramming without tears. *Society*, **17 (3)**, 34-38.

Levine E.M. (1980b). Rural communes and religious cults: Refuges for middle-class youth. In S. C. Feinstein et al. (Eds), *Adolescent Psychiatry*, Vol. 8 (pp. 138-153). Chicago: University of Chicago

Levine, E.M. (1985). Religious cults: A social-psychiatric analysis In B. K. Kilbourne (Ed.), *Scientific research and new religions : Divergent perspectives* (pp. 114-122). San Francisco: Pacific, Association for Advancement of Science.

Levine, S. V. (1979, 7 Nov.).The role of psychiatry in the phenomenon of cults. *Canadian Journal of Psychiatry*, **24**, 593-603.

218

Levine, S.V. (1980). The role of psychiatry in the phenomenon of cults. In S.C. Feinstein, et al. (Eds.). *Adolescent Psychiatry*, Vol. 8 (pp. 123-137). Chicago: University of Chicago Press.

Levine, S.V. (1981). Cults and mental health: Clinical conclusions. *Canadian Journal of Psychiatry*, **26**, 534-539.

Levine, S.V. (1984). *Radical departures: Desperate detours to growing up*. Chicago : University of Chicago Press.

Levine, S.V., & Slater, N.E. (1976). Youth and contemporary religious movements: Psychosocial findings. *Canadian Psychiatric Association Journal*, **21**, 411-420.

Lewin, K. (1948). *Resolving Social Conflicts*, (G.W. Lewin, Ed.). New York: Harper.

Lewin, K. (1951). *Field theory in social science* (D. Cartwright, Ed.). New York: Harper.

Lewis, T.N. (1979, May). Apostates in convention. *Midstream*, **25** (5) 46-48.

Lifton, R.J. (1961). *Thought reform and the psychology of totalism: A study of "brainwashing" in China*. New York: W.W. Norton.

Lipson, J.G. (1980). Jews for Jesus: An illustration of syncretism. *Anthropological Quarterly*, **53 (2)**, 101-110.

Loewenstein, R. (1951). *Christians and Jews: A psycho-analytical study*. (V. Damman, Trans.) New York: International Universities Press.

Lofland, J. (1977). *Doomsday cult*, enlgd. ed. New York: Irvington Publishers.

London Jewish Chronicle (1858-1865) . Newspaper.

London Times (1853-1866). Newspaper.

Lustiger, A. (1979, March 23). Eroding Judaism from within. *Jewish Exponent.* Philadelphia.

Lyles, J.C. (1977, May 11). Letting go: Everybody has the right to be wrong. *Christian Century,* **94,** 451-453.

Mahler, R. (1971). *A History of Modern Jewry,* Vol. I, 1780-1815. New York: Shocken.

Maitre, J. (1981, January). Ideologie religieuse, conversion mystique et symbiose, mère-enfant. Le case de Thérèse Martin (1875-1899). *Archives de Sciences Sociales des Religions,* **26,** 65-100.

Marcia, J.E. (1966). Development and validation of ego-identity status. *Journal of Personality and Social Psychology,* **3,** 551-558.

Marin, P. (1979, Feb.) Spiritual obedience. *Harper's,* **258,** 43-58.

Maritain, R. (1946, Jan.). Shock of conversion. *(New) Catholic World,* **269.** 364-365.

Maslow, A. (1954). *Toward a psychology of being.* Princeton, N. J. : Van Nostrand.

McGowan, T. (1979, Jan.-Feb.). The Unification Church. *The Ecumenist,* 273.

Meerloo, J.A.M. (1956).*The rape of the mind.* New York : World Publishing.

Melton, J.G. & Moore, R.L. (1982). *The cult experience: Responding to new religious pluralism.* New York: Pilgrim Press.

Miller, J.B.M. (1971). Children's reactions to the death of a parent: a review of the psychoanalytic literature. *Journal of the American Psychoanalytic Association,* **19,** 697-719.

Morris, H.C., & Morris, L.M. (1978), Power and purpose: correlates to conversion. *Psychology,* **15 (4),** 15-22.

Newman, T.I. (1945). *A chief rabbi becomes a Catholic.* New York: Renascence Press.

Nicholi, A.M. (1974). A new dimension of the youth culture. *American Journal of Psychiatry,* **131,** 396-440.

Ostow, M. (1975). Religion and psychiatry. In A. M. Freedman, H.I. Kaplan & F.J. Sadock (Eds.). *Comprehensive textbook of psychiatry,* 2nd ed., Vol. II (pp. 2529-2536). Baltimore: Williams and Wilkins .

Ostow, M. (1977). The psychologic determinants of Jewish identity. *Israel Annals of Psychiatry and Related Disciplines,* **15 (4),**313-335.

Ostow, M. (1981). Private communication.

Ostow, M. (1982). The hypomanic personality. In M. Ostow (Ed.). *Judaism and psychoanalysis* (pp.219-230). New York: Ktav.

Paloutzian, R.F., Jackson, S.L., & Crandall, J.E. (1978). Conversion experience, belief system, and personal and ethical attitudes.*Journal of Psychology and Theology,* **6 (4),** 266-275.

Parker, M.G. (1978, Jan.). Dimensions of religious conversion during adolescence. *Dissertation Abstracts International*, **38 (708): 3371B**.

Parucci, D.J. (1968). Religious conversion, A theory of deviant behavior. *Sociological Analysis*, **29**, 144-154.

Pattison, E.M. (1980). Religious youth cults: alternative healing social networks. *Journal of Religion and Health*, **19**, 275-286.

Peele, S. & Brodsky, A. (1975). *Love and addiction*. New York: Taplinger Publishing Co.

Pelcovits, N.S. (1947, Feb.). What about Jewish antisemitism? A prescription to cure self-hatred. *Commentary*, **3**, 118-125.

Pollack, M. (1980). *Mandarins, Jews and missionaries: The Jewish experience in the Chinese Empire*. Philadelphia: Jewish Publication Society.

Pogue, J. (1982, August 1). The mysterious ways of the Way. *Philadelphia Inquirer*.

Prince, M. (1906). The psychology of sudden religious conversion.*Journal of Abnormal Psychology*, **1 (1)**, 52-54.

Prince, M. (1913). *The dissociation of a personality*, 2nd ed. New York: Longman Green.

Ratisbonne, A.M. (1842). *Lettre de M. A. Ratisbonne sur sa conversion*. Paris.

Ratisbonne, M.T. (1868). *La question juive*. Paris.

Ratisbonne, M.T. (1878). *Réponses aux questions d'un Israélite de notre temps*. Paris, Brussels.

Ratisbonne, M.T. (1903). *Père Marie-Théodore Ratisbonne, fondateur de la société des prêtres et de la congrégation des religieuses de Notre-Dame de Sion.*, 2 Vols. Paris.

Rausch, D.A. (1979, May). Jews evangelized, messianic Jews. *Midstream*, 36-41.

Rémond, R. (1976). *L'anti-clericalisme en France de 1815 à nos jours.* Paris: Fayard..

Return of the Finaly brothers (1953, July 11). *America*, **89**, 370.

Ruether, R. (1974). *Faith and fraticide.* New York: Seabury Press. *Revue de deux Mondes* (1858). Journal

Rice, B. (1976, Jan.). Messiah from Korea: Honor thy Father Moon. *Psychology Today*, **9 (8)**, 36-47.

Robbins, T. (1969). Eastern mysticism and the resocialization of drug users. *Journal for the Scientific Study of Religion,* **8 (2)**, 308-317.

Robbins,T. (1979). Cults and the therapeutic state. *Social Policy,* **10 (1)**, 42-46.

Robbins, T., & Anthony, D. (1972). Getting straight with Meher Baba. *Journal for the Scientific Study of Religion,* **11 (2)**.

Robbins, T., & Anthony, D. (1982). Deprogramming, brainwashing, and the medicalization of deviant religious groups. *Social Problems*, **29**, 283-297.

Rochford, E.B., Jr. (1985). *Hare Krishna in America.* New Brunswick: Rutgers University Press.

Rosen, D. (1987, May 15). Is sainthood a dubious honor? *Jewish Exponent*, pp.31, 38.

Rosenbloom, J.R. (1978). *Conversion to Judaism: From the Biblical period to the present*. Cincinnati: Hebrew Union Press.

Ross, M., McFarland, C., & Fletcher, G.J.O. (1981). The effect of attitude on the recall of personal histories. *Journal of Personality and Social Psychology, 40*, 627-634.

Roth, C. (1947). *A history of the Marranos*, rev. ed. Philadelphia: Jewish Publication Society.

Royse, D.D. (1904). The psychology of Saul's conversion. *Journal of Religious Psychology, 1*, 143-154.

Rudin, A.J. (1978). Jews and Judaism in Reverend Moon's *Divine Principle*. In I.L.Horowitz (Ed.), *Science, sin, and scholarship* (pp.74-83). Cambridge, MA: The M.I.T. Press.

Salzman, L. (1953). The psychology of religious and ideological conversion. *Psychiatry, 16*, 177-187.

Salzman, L. (1966). Types of religious conversion. *Pastoral Psychology, 17*, 8-20; 66.

Sanua, V.D. (1974). The contemporary Jewish family: A review of the social science literature. *Journal of Jewish Communal Service, 50 (4)*, 297-312.

Sargant, W. (1957). *Battle for the mind: a physiology of conversion and brainwashing*. London: William Heinemann.

224

Schafer, S. (1974). The beginnings of "victimology." In I. Dropkin & E.Viano (Eds.), *Victimology*. Lexington, MA: Lexington Books.

Scharff, G. (1982). Autobiography of a former Moonie. *Center Magazine*, **(2)**, 14-17.

Schein, E., Schein, I., & Barker, C.H. (1971). *Coercive persuasion*. New York: W.W. Norton.

Schwartz, L.L. (1982). Therapy with families of cult members. In S. Gurman (ed.), *Questions and answers in the practice of family therapy*, Vol. 2 (pp.78-81). New York: Brunner/ Mazel.

Schwartz, L.L. (1983). Family therapy and families of cult members. *International Journal of Family Therapy*, **5 (3)**, 168-178.

Schwartz, L.L. (1986). Parental responses to their children's cult membership. *Cultic Studies Journal*, **3**, 187-200.

Schwartz, L.L. & Isser, N. (1979). Psychohistorical perception of involuntary conversion. *Adolescence*, **14**, 352-360.

Schwartz, L.L. & Isser, N. (1981). Some involuntary conversion techniques. *Jewish Social Studies*, **43 (1)**, 1-10.

Schwartz, L.L. & Kaslow, F.W. (1981). The cult phenomenon. *Marriage and Family Review*, **4 (3/4)**, 3-30.

Schwartz, L.L. & Kaslow, F.W. (1979). Religious cults, the individual, and the family. *Journal of Marital and Family Therapy*, **5 (2)**, 15-26.

Schwartz, L.L. & Zemel, J.L. (1980). Religious cults : Family concerns and the law. *Journal of Marital and Family Therapy*, 301-308.

Scobie, G.E.W. (1975). *Psychology of religion.* London: B. T. Botsford, Ltd.

Scroggs, J.R. & Douglas, W.G.T. (1977). Issues in the psychology of conversion. In H.N. Malony (Ed.), *Perspectives in the psychology of religion* (pp. 254-265). Grand Rapids, Mich. : Wm. B. Erdmans, .

Scult, M. (1973, January). English mission to the Jews, conversion in the age of emancipation. *Jewish Social Studies,* **35,** 3-17.

Shaffir, W. (1978). Witnessing as identity consolidation: the case of the Lubavitcher chassidim. In H. Mol (Ed.). *Identity and religion* (pp. 39-57). Beverly Hills, CA. : Sage.

Shapiro, E. (1977). Destructive cultism. *American Family Physician,* **381.** 80-85.

Shupe, A.D., Jr. & Bromley, D.G. (1980). *New vigilantes: Deprogrammers, anticultists, and the new religions.* Beverly Hills, CA : Sage.

Silverman, P.R., & Silverman, S.M. (1979). Withdrawal in bereaved children. In B. Schoenberg, A.C. Carr, D. Peretz, & A.H. Kutscher (Eds), *In loss and grief: Psychological management in medical practice* (pp. 208-214). New York: Columbia University Press.

Simmonds, R.B. (1977a). Conversion or addiction. *American Behavioral Scientist,* **20,** 909-924.

Simmonds, R.B. (1977b). The people of the Jesus movement. *Dissertation Abstracts.* **38 (2-B)**, 969-970.

Simos, B.G. (1979). *A time to grieve: Loss as a universal human experience.* New York : Family Association of America

Singer, M.T. (1979a). Coming out of the cults. *Psychology Today,* **12 (8)**, 72-82.

Singer, M.T. (1979b). Paper presented at the Friends Hospital Conference, Philadelphia.

Sklare, M. (1978). The conversion of the Jews. *Commentary,* **56 (3)**, 44-53.

Sobel, B.Z. (1974). *Hebrew Christianity: The thirteenth tribe.* New York: John Wiley.

Sontag, F. (1979). *Sun Myung Moon and the Unification Church.* Nashville : Abingdon Press.

Spero, M.H. (1977). Cults: Some theoretical and practical perspectives. *Journal of Jewish Communal Service,* **54**, 330-338.

Spero, M.H. (1980). The stimulus value of religion to cultic and penitent personality types. *Journal of Psychology and Judaism,* **4 (3)**, 161-170.

Spero, M.H. (1982). Psychotherapeutic procedures with cult devotees. *Journal of Nervous and Mental Disease,* **170**.

Spero, M.H. (1984). Some pre- and post-treatment characteristics of cult devotees. *Perceptual and Motor Skills,* **58**, 749-750.

Stark, R. & Bainbridge, W. S. (1980). Networks of faith: Interpersonal bonds and recruitment to cults and sects. *American Journal of Sociology,* **85 (6),** 1376-1395.

Stark R. & Bainbridge, W.S. (1981). Secularization and cult formation in the jazz age. *Journal for the Scientific Study of Religion,* **20,** 360-372.

Stoner, C. & Parke, J.A. (1977). *All Gods children: Salvation or slavery?* Radnor, PA : Chilton Book Co.

Streiker, L.D. (1971). *The Jesus trip.* Nashville: Abingdon Press.

Szajkowski, Z. (1965). Simon Deutz: traitor or French patriot? *Journal of Jewish Social Studies,* **16,** 53-67.

Taylor, B. (1978). Recollection and membership: Converts' talk and the ratiocination of commonality. *Sociology,* **12 (2),** 316-324.

Thompson, D. (1946). Recent conversions. *Commonwealth,* **43,** 597.

Time (1982, December 27), pp.50-56.

Tipton, S.M. (1982). The moral logic of alternative religion. *Daedalus,* **(1),** 185-214.

Toch, H. (1965). *The social psychology of social movements.* Indianapolis : Bobb-Merrrill.

Toynbee, A.J. (1947). *A study of history* (an abridgement of Vol. I-III by D. C. Somerville). New York and London.

228

Travisano, R.V. (1970). Alternation and conversion as qualitatively different transformations. In G. P. Stone & H. A. Faberman (Eds.), *Social psychology through symbolic interaction* (pp. 594-606). Waltham, MA : Zerox College Publishing Co.

Tucker, R.C. (1968). The theory of charismatic leadership. *Daedalus*, **97**, 731-756.

Underwood, A.C. (1925). *Conversion: Christian and non-Christian*. London: George Allen and Unwin.

Univers Israélite (1858-1864, 1860-1861). Newspaper.

Unterleider, J.T., & Wellisch, D.K. (1979a). Coercive persuasion (brainwashing), religious cults, and de-programming. *American Journal of Psychiatry*, **136 (3)**, 279-282.

Unterleider, J.T., & Wellisch, D.K. (1979b). Cultism, thought control and deprogramming : Observations on a phenomenon. *Psychiatric Opinion*, **16 (1)**, 10-15.

Vatican Secretariat for Non-Christians. (1986). Sects or new religious movements: A pastoral challenge. *Cultic Studies Journal*, **3**, 93-116.

Vegh, C. (1984). *I didn't say good-bye* (R. Schwartz, trans.). New York : E. P. Dutton.

Vérité Israélite (1861). Newspaper.

Volli, G. (1960). *Il caso Mortara nel prima centenario*. Roma.

Wallis, R. (1975). Scientology: Therapeutic cult to religious sect. *Sociology*, **9 (1)**, 89-104.

Wallis, R. (1979). *Salvation and protest: Studies of social and religious movements.* New York: St. Martin's Press.

Warshaw, R. (1979). Anybody's kid: Cults and the Jewish connection. *Expo,* **5 (2),** 36-40; 103-113.

Weber, M. (1956). *The sociology of religion* (E. Fischoff, trans.). Boston: Beacon Press.

Weightman, J.M. (1981). Peoples Temple: Creation of a new reality. Paper presented at the annual meeting of the Society for the Scientific Study of Religion, Baltimore.

Weininger, B. (1955). The interpersonal factor in the religious experience. *Psychoanalysis,* **4,** 27-44.

Weinstein, F.S. (1985). *A hidden childhood* (B.L.Kennedy, Trans.). New York: Hill and Wang.

West, L.J., & Singer, M.T. (1980). Cults, quacks, and non-professional psychotherapies. In H.B. Kaplan, A.M. Freedman, and B.J. Sadock (Eds.). *Comprehensive Textbook of Psychiatry,* Vol. 3, 3rd ed. (pp.3245-3258). Baltimore: Williams and Wilkins.

Wilson, W.P. (1972). Mental health benefits of religious salvation. *Diseases of the Nervous System,* **33,** 382-386.

Wright, S.A. (1984). Post-involvement attitudes of voluntary defectors from controversial new religious movements. *Journal for the Scientific Study of Religion,* **23,** 172-182.

Wright, S.A., & Piper, E.S. (1986). Families and cults: Familial factors related to youth leaving or remaining in deviant religious groups. *Journal of Marriage and the Family,* **48,** 15-25.

230

Yamamoto, J.I. (1977). *The Puppet Masters*. Downers Grove, Ill.: Intervarsity Press.

Zablocki, B., & Aidala, A. (1980). The varieties of communitarian ideology. In B. Zablocki (Ed.), *Alienation and Charisma: A Study of Contemporary American Communes* (pp. 189-246). New York: The Free Press.

Zoller, I. (1954). *Before the dawn*. London: Sheed and Ward.